Prayer That Works

BY KENNEDY OCHIENG OKELLO

Prayer That Works

Cover design by Mark Reynolds
Main cover photo by Kaarin Swanson
Wheat in Hand Photo: Jim Shroyer, Kansas State University
Working the Field Photo: Council of Churches in Sierra Leone
Sugar Cane Photo: Kaarin Swanson

Edited By:
Janice Busboom, Scott Linklater, Dan Smith, Virginia Linklater, Julie McAleer
Printed in the United States by Lulu.com
All Bible Quotations are in New International Version (NIV) unless indicated otherwise.

ISBN #: 978-0-6151-4440-5

Foreword and Introduction

From one point of view, guns, cockroaches, and half-cooked goat describe the trip. I have never sweated so much in my life. At 5:30 am, the loud speakers mounted on the Mosques start their call to prayer – a chilling sound to a naïve westerner. It is all new to me. To Ken, however, this is daily life in Garissa.

After a 7 hour bus ride, we arrive in Dadaab, a dust-bowl invisible to the world, where the United Nations has set up refugee camps for Somalis fleeing civil war and chaos. It is literally on frontlines of Christianity. Sleeping in a police compound fenced by barbed-wire and surrounded by 150,000 Muslim refugees, a highly educated man sacrifices creature-comforts to share the good news of Jesus Christ, and train others to do the same, with hardly more than a Bible. No kudos, very little encouragement, little money, constant danger, disease, and yet full of faith. He is sent by God to do a job. He believes firmly that there is no limit to the power of the Great Sender! This is the essence of Ken and Eunice: faith in prayer, obedience in action.

In December of 2004, I traveled to Kenya to meet a man named Kennedy Ochieng and to find out what he was doing to serve God. I found not only a good friend, but a person that I deeply respect and admire. The work that he and his wife do is amazing...period. I spent time in Garissa and Dadaab, and can attest to his heart for people and his faith in the power of prayer. Without faith in the power of God, Ken's work would fail and his life would be compromised. Because of his faith in God and the power of prayer, he not only survives in the desert, but also makes a tremendous impact for the Kingdom of God. Ken is laying down his life that Jesus might be known. Obedience and prayer have become a potent combination.

Ken will not brag, beg, or bargain. He is there to do a job, and prayer is the basis for his effectiveness. *Prayer That Works* is not theoretical. It is an explanation of what works, proven through experience and results. It will connect you to some basic principals and methods that will transform the way you look at prayer, changing it from a passive discipline to an active weapon.

I hope that you will be blessed by the contents in these pages, and that your faith in God will increase. Let Ken's faith spread to your heart and let his methods inspire you to action. We live in a world that needs Jesus and His saving grace. Let this book compel you to pray to the Lord of the harvest and move you to pick up your cross and follow Christ. When He is for us, who can be against us!

Scott Linklater
Pullman Foursquare Church
Pullman, Washington

Prayer and Desperation

Desperate people do strange things to get what they want. I remember hearing a story of a man who was in serious need of a job. The man was married and they had just been blessed with a baby. There was no food for either the couple or the baby. The man decided that he would take whichever job came his way. He searched around but he could not get any job. Finally he visited a zoo and requested to be given any job available to which the boss looked at him and laughed. "I do not think you will manage the job", he said. The man responded by saying that he was ready for whatever job. The boss started explaining to him the nature of the job. One of the monkeys that had been a major attraction had died. The man was told that his job would be to dress like that monkey and entertain the customers just like a real monkey. So he was taken through orientation. He was desperate and would do anything. One day when hundreds of people had gathered to watch the famous monkey, the monkey (who was actually a man) started jumping from one tree to another, one branch to another and so forth. Unfortunately because of fatigue, the 'monkey' fell down into a den of lions. People were so keen to watch what was going to happen between the 'monkey' and the lion. The true picture of the 'monkey' had to come out when confronted by the 'real lion'. The 'monkey' was starting to scream for help when surprisingly the 'real lion' whispered to the 'monkey' –"Man, shut up or we will both lose our jobs!" The man was desperate for a job and he got it!

I see a pattern in the Bible where God comes through for those who have reached what I prefer to call the "irreducible minimum." The principal of the "irreducible minimum" is simple. God will wait for you to explore all available options until you have exhausted all of them. After you have failed and realized that there is no solution to your problem, then He shows up and solves it for you. This is the marriage of prayer and desperation.

God will not come into the picture if you are trusting in the money you have in the bank or trusting in your friends or parents to help you out. When you have finally come to the end of yourself then that is when God tells you "bring it to me."

Hannah & Desperation

The story of Hannah is a good example of desperation for an answer from God. Elkanah was a good husband and took care of Hannah. He showed her love and was there for her but Hannah was confronted by a painful experience of barrenness.

In the present day, barrenness is not the same issue because couples sometimes even decide to not have children. Economic issues and modern approaches to life have made it necessary to redefine different issues. In Hannah's time, barrenness was interpreted to mean a curse. Every person derived pleasure in knowing that even if they died, their generation would continue to live. In Hannah's case, barrenness meant that she would not have a generation after her and there was nothing as painful as this. Hannah did not see the essence of living without children of her own. Hannah probably explored other options available to cure the problem. Maybe she spent lots of money seeking for treatment so her womb would open up, but all the options she tried failed.

You see, every time Hannah got excited about anything, there was always this thorn in the flesh shouting loud in her mind "but you do not have a baby!" This voice would frustrate her and make her lonely. I have come to realize that you can be lonely even if there are people around you. Some young people get married for the wrong reason of running away from loneliness. The truth of the matter is that you can be lonely even in marriage. Elkanah seemed not to have realized what Hannah was going through.

In my own village, barren women are despised and alienated from the rest of the people. People have the mistaken idea that in order for you to be barren you must have sinned. This concept worsens the situation for the barren woman. People always like associating themselves with successful people or those that look blessed. In our day, premiums are placed on superficial value systems, stating that your value in life is dependent on the kind of car you drive, the type of house you own, the dress you put on and the type of people you hang around with. This value system can be so stressful especially if we do not measure up to the standard set by men. Hannah was a victim of wrong value systems of her day.

The person who took upon herself the responsibility of irritating Hannah was none other than her co-wife Peninnah. It is always difficult for co-wives to get along well for a number of reasons. Both are competing for the same resources the man has and are trying their best to make sure that they win the love of the husband. The case of Hannah and Peninnah was not an exception of rivalry between co-wives.

And because the Lord had closed her womb, her rival kept provoking her in order to irritate her. This went on year after year. Whenever Hannah went up to the house of the Lord, her rival provoked her till she wept and would not eat. ~1 Samuel 1:6-7

From this scripture, I realize that people can be so heartless to the extent that they do not sympathize with situations of others regardless of how serious it is. Instead of some people sympathizing with your situation, they would want your situation to finish you totally. Surely, Peninnah had children and the best she could have done was to sympathize and encourage Hannah. Think about the 'Peninnahs' of your life, those people or situations that have drawn a battle line against you and are ready to finish you. We learn something from Hannah in this scripture: you should not allow people or situations to overcome you or make you look down upon yourself. Instead you should let them move you to prayer.

Stay Positive

Someone once said that pain is one of the weapons God uses to get our attention when we are too busy for him. Situations or people that are against us should drive us to prayer and not away from God.

The 'co-wife' could be a colleague at a place of work who is always giving a wrong report about you so you can be sacked. It could be a fellow member of the choir who is always harping about your weakness and inability to sing well. My desire is to encourage you to develop the right attitude and to see that those things you are going through are wake-up calls for prayer. In Hannah's case, she was pushed beyond the limit. It is like an elastic band: it will only stretch to a given level and if the tension is too much, it gives way because that is the end of its elasticity. Hannah had reached the irreducible minimum and something had to be done in her situation now or never.

Once when they had finished eating and drinking in Shiloh, Hannah stood up. Now Eli the priest was sitting on a chair by the doorpost of the Lord's temple. In bitterness of soul Hannah wept much and prayed to the Lord. And she made a vow, saying, "O Lord Almighty, if you will only look upon your servant's misery and remember me, and not forget your servant but give her a son, then I will give him to the Lord for all the days of his life, and no razor will ever be used on his head." As she kept on praying to the Lord, Eli observed her mouth. Hannah was praying in her heart, and her lips were moving but her voice was not heard. Eli thought she was drunk and said to her, "How long will you keep on getting drunk? Get rid of your wine". ~1 Samuel 1:9-14

You see, people will confuse the issue when you pour yourself out unreservedly to the Lord. People have a way they expect prayers to be made but when you go against this expectation, they will say you are drunk, confused, or pretending to be all sorts of things. For Hannah, getting a baby was the priority and she was pleading for the answer regardless of what name she was labeled along the way.

I want you to look at the response of this prayer warrior in the midst of the accusations she faced: *Not so, my Lord," Hannah replied, "I am a woman who is deeply troubled. I have not been drinking wine or beer; I was pouring out my soul to the Lord. Do not take your servant for a wicked woman; I have been praying here out of my great anguish and grief.* ~1 Samuel 1:15-16

Hannah did not dismiss Eli for referring to her as drunk. Negative responses to negative people will only rob us of the answer we so desperately need. Prayer offered out of a great anguish will always attract God's attention. Prayer that is carelessly uttered for the sake of prayer will not yield result. In Hannah's case, we see the result of a prayer made out of anguish and grief.

Wait on the Lord

Early the next morning they arose and worshipped before the Lord and then went back to their home at Ramah. Elkanah lay with Hannah, his wife, and the Lord remembered her. So in the course of time Hannah conceived and gave birth to a son. She named him Samuel, saying, "Because I asked the Lord for him." ~1 Samuel 1:19-20

Despite our desperation for an answer, it is important that we wait for God's timing. God's timing is the best for us. From the text, Hannah's prayer was answered but only in the "course of time". We should maintain patience while waiting for an answer. The world we live in will always seek to drive us to be anxious. God's word tells us: *Do not be anxious about anything, but in everything, by prayer and petition, with thanksgiving, present your requests to God.* ~Philippians 4:6

One of the big problems in our time is that we have been taught 'quick fix' habits. If we want coffee then there is instant coffee; if it is food, fast foods sell the most. We want everything really fast. When it comes to prayer, we must wait on God's timing and not our own. The problem is that we always want answers *now* and yet God may have reasons why we ought to wait. It could be that God wants you to grow to maturity before he can entrust you with that blessing you have been praying for.

My son Timothy is fond of asking me to give him my car so he can drive. It would be real madness if I were to succumb to this request since the fellow is only three years old. My love for him restrains me from giving him the car at that age because it will end up harming him. God's love for you will make him not give that answer you want because he knows it will bring you problems. Remember that his blessings add no sorrow.

It is important to take note that the devil will always seek to take advantage of our desperation for an answer from God. He might bring your way something that resembles the answer you were waiting for. It is unfortunate that many people have fallen into the trap of the enemy because they wanted an answer quickly.

And no wonder, for Satan himself masquerades as an angel of light. ~2 Corinthians 11:14

It makes sense to evaluate whether your answer is one from the Lord or a concoction from the enemy to meet your unquenchable quest for an answer. It is great wisdom to engage the brake and slow down whenever you are tempted to speed.

A person shared with me how he would be confronted by an unfriendly dog everyday as he came home from work. This kept going on for days. The dog would run after his car barking loudly at him and seemed to derive pleasure in this habit. One day as he was driving home, this same crazy dog started pursuing him in earnest. God whispered in the ear of this man telling him to engage the brake. He did and the dog, unaware that the brake had been engaged, rammed into the car and lost a number of teeth. The dog never tried to pursue the car again. My point is that you should not allow yourself to be so anxious for an answer that you forget to brake and reason.

The Philistines assembled to fight Israel with three thousand chariots, six thousand charioteers, and soldiers as numerous as the sand on the seashore. They went up and camped at Micmash, east of Beth Aven. When the men of Israel saw that their situation was critical and that their army was hard pressed, they hid in caves and thickets, among the rocks, and in pits and cisterns. Some Hebrews even crossed the Jordan to the land of Gad and Gilead. Saul remained at Gilgal, and all the troops with him were quaking with fear. He waited seven days, the time set by Samuel; but Samuel did not come to Gilgal, and Saul's men began to scatter. So he said, "Bring me the burnt offering and the fellowship offering." And Saul offered up the burnt offering. ~1 Samuel 13:5-9

Saul thought that the answer took too long and decided to produce one. Before condemning Saul, it is important to take note of his predicament. His enemies, the Philistines, who were feared in war, had assembled themselves to fight the Israelites. The situation of the Israelites was critical and the army hard pressed—people were in fact running away. We realize that the above situation should not justify anyone to push things to work for himself. It is very tempting to manufacture an answer for yourself in your own timing after you have prayed.

Saul thought it had taken too long to get an answer. What happens when you accelerate the process of getting an answer?

"*Just as he finished making the offering, Samuel arrived, and Saul went out to greet him. "What have you done?" asked Samuel.* ~1 Samuel 13:10-11a

Your answer is almost always around the corner whenever you are tempted to settle for less. *"You acted foolishly," Samuel said* (1 Samuel 13:13a). Settling for anything less than an answer from God is foolish. You will not prosper if you are the type that is hasty to get answers that are not from God.

But now your kingdom will not endure; the Lord has sought out a man after his own heart and appointed him leader of his people, because you have not kept the Lord's command. ~ 1 Samuel 13:14

Another example of people who were desperate for an answer is the two blind men as told in Matthew.

As Jesus and his disciples were leaving Jericho, a large crowd followed him. Two blind men were sitting by the roadside, and when they heard that Jesus was going by, they shouted, "Lord, Son of David, have mercy on us!" The crowd rebuked them and told them to be quiet, but they shouted all the louder, "Lord, Son of David, have mercy on us!" Jesus stopped and called them. "What do you want me to do for you?" he asked. "Lord," they answered, "we want our sight." Jesus had compassion on them and touched their eyes. Immediately they received their sight and followed him. ~ Matthew 20:29-34

The truth of the matter is that the two blind men were tired of their situation and were desperate for a solution. Not even rebukes from the crowd would stop them from pleading for an answer.

Thankfulness

Another aspect that I want to bring together with desperation in prayer is that of thankfulness when our prayers are answered. The heart of desperation must be replaced with a heart of thankfulness after the prayer has been answered. A lot of people pray passionately for God to answer the cry of their heart only to forget after the answer has come.

A story is told of a man from my village who found a relative in Nairobi waiting for a bus. Because he was coming home and had a car, he decided to give a ride to the other person all the way home—this is almost a distance of 400 kilometers. After reaching home, the owner of the car watched in amazement as the relative left the car without any word of appreciation about the free lift he was given. Disgusted about this ungratefulness he called back his relative and requested him to get into the car briefly as if he wanted to remind him something he had forgotten about. The unsuspecting passenger got into the car unaware of what was awaiting him. Suddenly, the man ignited the car and hit the road all the way back to Nairobi (a distance of 400 kms.) to drop the ungrateful fellow at the point where he was picked up. This story is narrated in my village to encourage people to be thankful whenever they receive help from anyone.

Look at Hannah's response: *After he was weaned, she took the boy with her, young as he was, along with a three-year-old bull, an ephah of flour and a skin of wine, and brought him to the house of the Lord at Shiloh. When they had slaughtered the bull, they brought the boy to Eli, and she said to him, "As surely as you live, my lord, I am the woman who stood here beside you praying to the Lord. I prayed for this child, and the Lord has granted me what I asked of him. So now I give him to the Lord. For his whole life he will be given over to the Lord." And he worshipped the Lord there.* ~ 1 Samuel 1:24

The heart of gratefulness took Hannah back to the house of the Lord at Shiloh. Prayer warriors must be men and women with thankful hearts. Humanly speaking, you are more willing to help people who are grateful. Nobody wants to help people who will not even recognize the help they are receiving. Taking help as a right can be very discouraging to those who are offering it. I am a missionary in a part of the world where people have a wrong concept of the doctrine of predestination. According to these friends of mine, God has predestined things and they must happen per His will. Unlike the Christian doctrine of predestination where the will of man is taken into the equation, in this doctrine, man is reduced to a mere stooge. A person will just do something wrong and blame it on "Insha Allah" (God's will). It is always disheartening to me whenever I help one of the locals and they ignore me because according to them, God predestined that I would help at that time and that the help given was inevitable.

A prayer from a grateful heart will always attract God's attention.

Now on his way to Jerusalem, Jesus traveled along the border between Samaria and Galilee. As he was going into a village, ten men who had leprosy met him. They stood at a distance and called out in a loud voice, "Jesus,

Master, have pity on us!" When he saw them, he said, "Go, show yourselves to the priests." And as they went, they were cleansed. One of them, when he saw he was healed, came back, praising God in a loud voice. He threw himself at Jesus' feet and thanked him--and he was a Samaritan. Jesus asked, "Were not all ten cleansed? Where are the other nine? Was no one found to return and give praise to God except this foreigner?" ~Luke 17:11 – 18

Remember that all the ten lepers were praying for healing from the Lord. Their desperation for healing caused them not to be ashamed or afraid of anything as indicated by the loud voices they used as they pleaded for Jesus' intervention. All of them were healed but not all came back. They had been cleansed and never wanted to associate with anything called leprosy. They never went back to Jesus, perhaps because they never wanted people to know that they were the ones who had leprosy. Pride snatched thankfulness from them. But one man wanted God to be glorified through his healing. Jesus was amazed that the foreigner knew the secret as to why prayers are answered. The reason God will answer your prayer requests for healing, deliverance, prosperity, and restoration is so that the glory may rebound back to Him. When you pray for salvation of other people and they are saved, the kingdom of God is expanded and God is glorified. Hannah modeled a heart of thankfulness that all of us are supposed to imitate.

"Do not be anxious about anything, but in everything, by prayer and petition, with ***thanksgiving****, present your requests to God. And the peace*

of God, which transcends all understanding, will guard your hearts and your minds in Christ Jesus." ~Philippians 4:6-7

Prayer and Persistence

Prayer is hard work. We need to create quality time so we can pray. Over the years I have come to realize that immediately when you set to pray, there will be lots of things to discourage you from your prayers. Prayer time is the very time that a long time friend will appear, a child will begin crying for your attention, the boss will call you for an urgent meeting, the customer will send for you about a lucrative business deal and the list is endless.

It takes a focused man/woman to pray while other things vie for attention. The enemy understands the power of prayer and will use everything at his disposal to make sure that you do not pray. Many Christians are busy doing God's work without prayer--- this is dangerous. God's work must be done God's way. The only way to know His way is by going to him in prayer. Evangelism without prayer is like an explosive without a detonator.

A combination of evangelism and prayer blows off the roof of hell. We must persist in prayer and fight those forces that are fighting us to give up praying.

The Amalekites came and attacked the Israelites at Rephidim. Moses said to Joshua, "Choose some of our men and go out to fight the Amalekites. Tomorrow I will stand on top of the hill with the staff of God in my hands." So Joshua fought the Amalekites as Moses had ordered, and Moses, Aaron, and Hur went to the top of the hill. As long as Moses held up his hands, the Israelites were winning, but whenever he lowered his hands, the Amalekites were winning. When Moses' hands grew tired, they took a stone and put it under him and he sat on it. Aaron and Hur held his hands up - one on one side, one on the other - so that his hands remained steady till sunset. So Joshua overcame the Amalekite army with the sword. ~Exodus 17:8-13

Moses knew that the battle belonged to the Lord. Swords alone were not going to guarantee success. God needed to be involved so the Israelites could defeat their enemy. Joshua was busy fighting the physical battle while Moses was fighting it in the spiritual realm. Victory could only be manifested after Moses won the same battle in the spiritual world. We must learn to conquer battles in the spiritual realm before we can expect to win them in the natural.

For our struggle is not against flesh and blood, but against the rulers, against the authorities, against the powers of this dark world and against the spiritual forces of evil in the heavenly realms. ~Ephesians 6:12

Prayer is the tool that God has given us to overcome the evil one, hence the need to persist in it even when we do not feel like it. Remember we do not have to live by our feelings. Bill Bright (founder of Campus Crusade for Christ) wrote about feelings and expressed it in a diagram below:

The word of God is like the engine that drives the train (our Christian walk). Our faith in the truth of the word of God is the fuel that feeds the engine. Our feelings are to follow along just like the coach of the train. Depending on feelings is just like putting the donkey cart before the donkey. I am not trying to negate emotions or feelings in anyway. I find myself shedding tears many times when I am praying---and I believe it is okay. Jesus himself shed tears when he looked at Jerusalem and realized that the people were not ready in their day of visitation. What I am laboring to make clear is that feelings cannot supersede the truth of God's word and your faith in the truth.

Every time you set your heart to pray, the devil will bring feelings of tiredness, discouragement, unhappiness, etc. His intention is to stop you from praying. Obeying your feelings and giving up means that the enemy has won. Again, I need to point out that we also need to know when we are truly tired and need rest. The difference between winners and losers is simply that losers give up too easily. Usually, people give up at the eleventh hour just when they are about to receive the crown. Jesus modeled perseverance in prayer:

Then Jesus went with his disciples to a place called Gethsemane, and he said to them, "Sit here while I go over there and pray." He took Peter and the two sons of Zebedee along with him, and he began to be sorrowful and troubled. Then he said to them, "My soul is overwhelmed with sorrow to the point of death. Stay here and keep watch with me." Going a little farther, he fell with his face to the ground and prayed, "My Father, if it is possible, may this cup be taken from me. Yet not as I will, but as you will." Then he returned to his disciples and found them sleeping. "Could you men not keep watch with me for one hour?" he asked Peter. "Watch and pray so that you will not fall into temptation. The spirit is willing, but the body is weak." ~Matthew 26:36-41

Notice that Jesus' expectation was that his disciples were to persevere in prayer. The disciples failed by obeying their feelings of tiredness and sleeping. Take note that if there was somebody who was tired in this group, then it was Jesus, as it is indicated that his soul was overwhelmed with sorrow to the point of death. Jesus refused to let his problem drive him to sleep; instead he opted to pray. I propose to you that whenever situations or circumstances confront you, let them drive you to prayer and not to sleep. I am amazed at Jesus' resilience especially as indicated in Matthew 26:42-44. *He went away a second time and prayed, "My Father, if it is not possible for this cup to be taken away unless I drink it, may your will be done." When he came back, he again found them sleeping because their eyes were heavy. So he left them and went away once more and prayed the third time, saying the same thing.*

The above portion of scripture shows us a man who was fighting all odds to pray. He overcame the forces against him and prayed over and over again. If our Lord, who is the King of the universe, persevered in prayer, then we as his disciples should persevere all the more. Perseverance has fruit at the end of it all. A story is told of a competition between a tortoise and a hare. They were to run a race for some kilometers. The hare started the race very fast and left the tortoise far behind. She then realized that her competitor was too weak so she decided to sleep a little bit because she thought the Tortoise could not catch up with her. She slept longer than expected. When she woke up, the Tortoise at her slow, steady speed had persevered in the race through the finishing line and received a crown as a reward.

Jesus' perseverance was serious and costly as recorded in Luke 22:44, *And being in anguish, he prayed more earnestly, and his sweat was like drops of blood falling to the ground.* We are talking about persevering until sweat begins looking like blood!

Look at Jesus' parable of the persistent widow in Luke 18:1–8. *Then Jesus told his disciples a parable to show them that they should always pray and not give up. He said: "In a certain town there was a judge who neither feared God nor cared about men. And there was a widow in that town who kept coming to him with the plea, "Grant me justice against my adversary." For some time he refused. But finally he said to himself, "Even though I do not fear God or care about men, yet because this widow keeps bothering me, I will see that she gets justice, so that she won't eventually wear me out with her coming!" And the Lord said, "Listen to what the unjust judge says. And will not God bring about justice for his chosen ones, who cry out to him day and night? Will he keep putting them off? I tell you, he will see that they get justice, and quickly."*

The unjust judge changed his mind because he could not cope with the persistence of the widow. God will always honor the persistence of his people as they cry to him day and night. The reason we have not seen great results for the things we have been praying is because our prayers have been casual and with no perseverance. Do you want to experience spiritual growth in your life? The answer is to persevere in prayer for growth. Do you want to experience restoration of your family or the family of a friend? Persevere in prayer, trusting God for restoration. Are you trusting God for healing upon your body or for a relative or friend? Persevere in prayer for healing. Friends, we can begin praying for the salvation of the so-called 'closed countries'. God has promised to answer us as we call on him day and night.

There once was an army that had invaded another land. The commander realized that their number was much smaller than their enemy's. He knew his people would run helter-skelter before the enemy because of fear. Being a person who knew the importance of perseverance, he decided to burn the only boat that they had used in crossing over to the battlefield. This way, he succeeded in destroying the vessel that would have transported cowards and those who easily give up. This army did not have any option but to fight, and sure enough they fought until they conquered their enemies. It is time learn to burn those bridges that would take you to the land of defeat.

Prayer and Discipline

Discipline is very important if someone is to succeed in anything. It is a proven fact that children who are disciplined are more successful academically than those who are not.

Discipline leads to character formation, which in turn leads to good habits. Kenyan athletes have dominated long distance running for many years. People enjoy watching them run tirelessly for a long time. The thing people do not know is the kind of discipline these athletes subject themselves to. I was raised up in Rift Valley (bedrock of Kenyan athletes) and I learned about the cost that these world record holders have to pay. I remember while in primary school how we would run a total of twelve kilometers to school and back home. There was no walking because you would end up arriving at school late and face the full wrath of the teacher on duty. In those days in Kenya, caning was allowed in schools and teachers seemed to derive great pleasure from administrating it. Nobody wanted to be late. The discipline of subjecting our bodies to the act of running twelve kilometers daily made our school, (Tinderet Primary School) produce great athletes. Kenyan athletes like Paul Tergat (New York marathon winner, 2005) and Catherine Ndereba (Boston marathon winner, 2005) run as many as fifty kilometers every day.

A good example of a man in the Bible who demonstrates the discipline of prayer is Daniel. Lets have a look at Daniel 6:4-11: *At this, the administrators and the satraps tried to find grounds for charges against Daniel in his conduct of government affairs, but they were unable to do so. They could find no corruption in him, because he was trustworthy and neither corrupt nor negligent. Finally these men said, "We will never find any basis for charges against this man Daniel unless it has something to do with the law of his God." So the administrators and the satraps went as a group to the king and said: "O King Darius, live forever!" The royal administrators, prefects, satraps, advisers and governors have all agreed that the king should issue an edict and enforce the decree that anyone who prays to any god or man during the next thirty days, except to you, O king, shall be thrown into the lions' den. Now, O king, issue the decree and put it in writing so that it cannot be altered - in accordance with the laws of the Medes and Persians, which cannot be annulled." So King Darius put the decree in writing. Now when Daniel learned that the decree had been published, he went home to his upstairs room where the windows opened toward Jerusalem. Three times a day he got down on his knees and prayed, giving thanks to his God, just as he had done before. Then these men went as a group and found Daniel praying and asking God for help.*

From this portion of scripture, we see that Daniel had cultivated the discipline of praying three times a day. Daniel would not compromise his time of prayer with anything else. It takes a lot of time and effort to cultivate a discipline, but the discipline can easily be messed up if the person is not focused.

Integrity

Other than discipline, prayer warriors must be people of integrity. I know many people who spend a lot of time praying but their lives are not in line with their confession. Prayer is communication with God. You cannot communicate with God genuinely without transformation in your inner being. People who spend quality time with God will always be changed to be more like Christ. The closer we get to God, the more we realize how sinful we are and are moved to repentance. The Pharisees only thought they were holy --- they were far from God and therefore unable to see their sinfulness. Daniel was a man of integrity. The administrators and the satraps could not find any ground for charges against him. They could not find any corruption in him. God's attention will always be attracted whenever the man of integrity opens up his mouth to call on him. We live in a time when many people are corrupt and it can be very difficult for people to get services without offering bribes. Christians have also succumbed to bribing their way for a job or bribing to win a business tender. Even obtaining documents like a driver's license, passport, and birth certificate has become so difficult that some believers have resorted to accepting the demands of the officer to be bribed. We should not expect answers to prayer if we are corruptible.

The reason why many of our prayers are not being answered is because we are not living right. We pray for an answer and yet try to bribe our way to get that answer. God will not honor this request. Daniel could have decided to obey the order so he could keep his plum job, but he did not. I have been especially disappointed by politicians who have been on fire for the Lord, but once they get into parliament, they begin to engage in corrupt practices and before long their testimony is gone. These same people end up driving non-believers far away from God because they can't see any difference between themselves and those who claim to have a relationship with God.

Corruption is not confined to politicians only. Religious leaders have also been trapped in the same quagmire. The love of money is a major contributor to corruption. The Bible is clear that the love of money is the root of all evil (1 Timothy 6:10). Money is not bad, but the love of it is. Many churches have split because of money issues. Some have even started ministries and churches as conduits for economic gains! If this is not a tragedy then what is? Things like misappropriation of funds should not even have a place in the body of Christ.

Another thing to take note of is that prayer warriors are trustworthy people. This means that they are dependable. Daniel was trustworthy and his word could be counted on. God will answer your prayer if you can be counted on to fulfill his purpose. The purpose of God should consume your thoughts and everything about you.

Negligent people do not make good prayer warriors. Prayer is hard work and lazy people cannot survive it. You cannot afford to take God's purposes casually and expect answers to your prayers. In order for you to sustain the discipline of prayer, you must identify where and when you will be praying. A lack of a strategic plan on how, when and where you will be praying is a very good avenue through which the enemy will give you excuses not to pray. Daniel's place of prayer was at home, in his upstairs room where the window opened toward Jerusalem. Daniel was praying for the people of Jerusalem and as he looked out of the window, he would be reminded to pray for the inhabitants of the city.

I will never forget an experience I had with a missionary from England. We both traveled to one of the 'closed countries'. We went into that country specifically to pray. God would have heard our prayers for that country even if we prayed in our own countries but going there was better because we received better direction on how to pray as we moved in that land and as we interacted with the people there. While in that country, we chose the tallest building where we could see every part of the city. The good thing was that the building was also at the highest elevation. We climbed on top of that building and had a great time calling on God on behalf of that country. Having a full view of the city revealed to us many prayer points. I encourage you to be sensitive to what your eyes see—it could be a way of God telling you to lift those things to him in prayer.

Priority

It is important that you choose a place that keeps you away from interference.

In Africa, the concept of time is still alien to many people. People will visit any time they are free without booking an appointment. To worsen the situation, the same people sit talking about irrelevant things for a whole three hours. As believers, we are told in the Bible to redeem the time because the days are evil (Ephesians 5:16). We cannot afford to spend time talking about where it is raining and how the livestock in the village are doing. It is time we learn to use the word we do not like to use: "No" We need to say "No" to things that are not a priority to us. People pleasers do not make good intercessors because they spend their time pleasing men at the expense of praying.

If you do not have many options of a place to pray then your bedroom could be a solution. Make sure that your children and spouse are aware of your prayer place and time so they do not distract you. If the house is too tiny for privacy of prayer then you can look for a quiet place within your neighborhood.

Jesus used to withdraw from the multitude and go to a place of solitude.

Immediately Jesus made the disciples get into the boat and go on ahead of him to the other side, while he dismissed the crowd. After he had dismissed them, he went up on a mountainside by himself to pray. When evening came, he was there alone… ~Matthew 14:22-23

Jesus wanted to have communion with the Father, and the best way for him to go about it was by being alone. What you are in public depends on what you are in private. If your private life is not ordered, do not expect your public life to be ordered. Some people try to give a show of what they are not in public, but it is just a matter of time before their private life begins to manifest publicly.

Daniel had the habit of locking himself in the closet. In accordance to Christ's teachings:

And when you pray, do not be like the hypocrites, for they love to pray standing in the synagogues and on the street corners to be seen by men. I tell you the truth, they have received their reward in full. When you pray, go into your room, close the door and pray to your Father, who is unseen. Then your Father, who sees what is done in secret, will reward you. ~Matthew 6:5-6

We live in a time when people like making shows of everything including prayer. Kenya has been in a drought that has caused food shortages in many parts of the country. What surprises me is that the people who were giving food to help relieve the situation always wanted major television stations to cover their exercise of helping the poor. It is an understatement to say that people love publicity. To avoid falling into the trap of 'publicity syndrome', we have to find a place of solitude in the presence of God.

It is in prayer closets that God has made his generals over the years. Unfortunately, this generation is commonly putting on public shows at the expense of staying in the closets. In Kenya for example, overnight prayers (known as Kesha) have been adopted by most churches. Kesha is usually done on Fridays because most people do not work on Saturdays and they can sleep in on Saturdays. I personally like Kesha but problems arise when we use Kesha as the only time for prayer. Many overnight prayers are also dominated by lots of teachings and testimonies. Those who do not have the opportunity to preach on a Sunday can do so on Fridays because there is 'plenty of time'. Teachings and testimonies are good but if a meeting is called for prayer then we must make sure that the actual praying takes most of the time. Besides overnight prayer and other prayer meetings, we must deliberately create time to be in our own prayer closets. Take note that hypocrites have wrong motives for praying—they place themselves strategically so all can see how prayerful they are. According to the Bible, these people should not expect any answer from God because the praise they get from men is enough reward for them (Matthew 6:5). Hypocrites can get respect from men because their long prayers endear them as servants of God. They will get respect and appreciation from men but that is all that there is for them because God will not answer their prayers. If you are making long prayers using long, spiritual sounding words so men can revere you, then your prayer is an exercise in futility. I encourage you to keep on evaluating your motives for prayer for this will determine whether your prayers are answered or not.

Frequency

The amount of time we spend praying is also important. The Bible encourages us to pray without ceasing (1 Thessalonians 5:17). I know many people around the world are so busy at their place of work that by the time they reach home, all they want to do is eat and sleep.

The dichotomization of our secular and spiritual realms or worlds is one thing that has done great damage to Christendom. We can be praying while working. They do not have to be loud prayers. The problem is that we have been taught that the work place is a purely secular place that needs pure secular talk—this is a lie. We are ambassadors at our place of work or business. We are to represent the kingdom of God all the time at every place. We are to keep in a mood of prayer even without saying a word.

Daniel made it his habit of praying three times a day. In East Africa and many parts of the world, people eat three meals a day—breakfast, lunch and supper. Whenever people miss a meal, they feel disappointed about it. Daniel knew that man was not to live on bread alone but by every word that proceeds from the mouth of God (Deuteronomy 8:3). Many people are disciplined in religiously taking three meals a day but find it difficult to spend time with God in prayer.

We have to spend a significant quantity of time praying. The quantity of time we spend doing something shows how much we prioritize it. Africans need to have a better concept of time, not acting like we have all the time in the world. We are not operating on our own time schedule but God's, hence the need to intentionally call on him. I am not advocating for taking long hours in prayer for the sake of it. In fact, the Bible is against the practice of repeating prayers just so you can be sure that you have been heard and become happy that you have spent a lot of time praying.

"And when you pray, do not keep on babbling like pagans, for they think they will be heard because of their many words. Do not be like them, for your Father knows what you need before you ask him." ~Matthew 6:7-8

We have many excuses as to why we are not prayerful. On the top of the list of excuses is the lack of time. We complain about lack of time yet we have time to attend sports, we have time to entertain visitors, we have time for sleeping that is not necessary, we have time to engage in vain arguments with other people, we have time to read secular books. The list is endless. There are things that we can easily do away with without any negative ramification.

We must create time for prayer just like we create time to eat. You will unlikely hear of somebody who has gone without food for three days because they did not have time to eat, yet we have many people who go for a week without prayer because they thought they did not have time.

Strategy

Jesus modeled prayer by creating time for prayer, choosing a time to pray and finding a place to pray.

Very early in the morning, while it was still dark, Jesus got up, left the house and went off to a solitary place, where he prayed. ~Mark 1:35

While others were enjoying their sleep and dreaming, Jesus was busy praying and thanking God for his mighty works and committing the day to God. God's people should not dare to face any day without committing it first to the Lord.

Jesus' time of prayer was very strategic—early morning when the mind is still fresh and the body strong. Jesus gave God his best time. We have to stop the habit of giving God the worst. Many people go to God when they are exhausted and before long they are in deep sleep.

Jesus also identified a place that was his closet.

Immediately Jesus made the disciples get into the boat and go on ahead of him to the other side, while he dismissed the crowd. After he had dismissed them, he went up on a mountainside by himself to pray. When evening came, he was there alone. ~Matthew 14: 22-23

Another scripture showing that Jesus preferred a mountainside as his closet is in Matthew 15:29: *Jesus left there and went along the Sea of Galilee. Then he went up on a mountainside and sat down.*

To Jesus, the mountainside was his closet. Jesus is the author of overnight prayer (kesha) as we see him pray throughout the night. The only difference between Jesus and our overnight prayers is that Jesus liked praying all alone. This is not to discourage church overnight prayers but to encourage believers to also have personal overnight prayers. Jesus spent a number of hours praying during the night—both quality and quantity are important.

I encourage those who have been praying for five minutes to consider increasing to ten minutes, those that have been praying for twenty minutes to try thirty minutes, and those that have been doing thirty minutes to go for one hour. You might struggle in the beginning with adjusting to a longer duration of time but you will adjust after a while. Our bodies are such that they are able to adjust to the discipline we give it.

If Jesus, who is our Lord and Savior, identified when and where to pray, you are no exception to this principle. This principle is not to make you a slave but it acts as a guide to enable you to enjoy your time of prayer.

Your time of prayer must be vibrant, dynamic and exciting. When you are praying, you are talking to your Father. Your Father wants to hear what you are excited about, what is bothering you and all other things that you are even afraid to share with your best friend.

In summary, be like Daniel, a man that was not corrupt, not negligent. He was disciplined in prayer and created a time and place for prayer. Jesus also identified a place and time for prayer. There is no reason why your prayer cannot work.

Prayer and Repentance

Prayer that gets answered is one that comes from a heart that has no unconfessed sin. Many of our prayers are not answered because we are harboring sin in our lives. As indicated earlier, prayer is communication with God. Our fellowship with God is very much a factor in whether our prayers are going to be answered or not.

The Bible tells us that the prayer of a sinner is like noise before God. Noise is irritating and all of us should do everything within our means to get rid of it. Noise does not make sense because the words are swallowed by noise. When the Bible says that the prayer of a sinner is like noise before God, it simply means that those prayers are irritating him and that they do not make sense to him. You are better off not praying if you harbor sin in your life.

Suppose you have wronged your father by doing what he told you not to do or by failing to do what he instructed you to do;

will it make sense for you to go to your father so he can assist you with what you need? The best thing to do in this situation is to fix the problem before you go to him with your lists of requests.

Chapter 9 of John narrates a story of a man born blind was healed by Jesus. Instead of giving God the glory, the Pharisees started to investigate the healing of this man. After several exchanges, the Pharisees realized that they were losing the argument with this man that was not trained in the law. They opted for insults, making statements such as "You are this fellow's disciple! We are disciples of Moses! But as for this fellow, we do not even know where he comes from." Now this new believer that had just experienced God's mighty healing, realized that these Pharisees were not as tough as he thought. He decided to take the Pharisees head on. He told them the truth that was like a punch in the stomach. In John 9:30-31, *The man answered, 'Now that is remarkable! You do not know where he comes from, yet he opened my eyes. We know that God does not listen to sinners. He listens to the godly man who does his will'.* Amazing, isn't it?

The Pharisees did not want to hear the truth but only what their itching ears wanted to hear. They believed that their prayers could be heard regardless of the spiritual condition of their hearts. It took a new believer to reveal to them the truth. The truth pierced their hearts and they reacted angrily as shown in John 9:34, *To this they replied, 'You were steeped in sin at birth; how dare you lecture us!' And they threw him out.*

Denial

We cannot continue in sin and expect God to answer our prayers. In Isaiah 1:15-16, *When you spread out your hands in prayer, I will hide my eyes from you; even if you offer many prayers, I will not listen. Your hands are full of blood; wash and make yourselves clean. Take your evil deeds out of my sight! Stop doing wrong.* In this passage, the Israelites were doing all kinds of evil deeds. There was a lack of justice as cases favored the rich at the expense of the poor, the widows and the orphans. There was oppression everywhere. The same oppressive and unjust people would spread out their hands in prayer. Prophet Isaiah made it clear to them that God does not listen to such prayers. Such prayers are a waste of time because they will not get attention from God. The same people also thought that many prayers would act as remedies for their sinful tendencies, but they were told that they would not.

Over the years, I have come to realize how people would rather go around issues than fix the problem. When a husband has wronged the wife, instead of asking for forgiveness, he would rather buy the wife new clothes or give her money for a new hairdo. Wives are not the exception. After wronging the husband, she would rather cook him a great meal than ask for forgiveness. My argument to you is that asking for forgiveness does not have a substitute; not our long prayers, not buying new clothes or fixing great meals.

Pride

Proud hearts find it difficult to ask for forgiveness. We've got to learn to be humble.

Submit yourselves, then, to God. Resist the devil, and he will flee from you. Come near to God and he will come near to you. Wash your hands, you sinners, and purify your hearts, you double-minded. Grieve, mourn and wail. Change your laughter to mourning and your joy to gloom. Humble yourselves before the Lord, and he will lift you up. ~James 4:7-10

God is known to oppose the proud. He also specializes in giving grace to those who are humble. Somebody once said that the world has never seen what God can do through the life of one person who is totally surrendered to him.

Young men, in the same way be submissive to those who are older. Clothe yourselves with humility toward one another, because, "God opposes the proud but gives grace to the humble." Humble yourselves, therefore, under God's mighty hand, that he may lift you up in due time. ~1 Peter 5:5-6

Remember that any form of good works cannot substitute for our wickedness. Listen to what the psalmist says in chapter 66:18-20, "*If I had cherished sin in my heart, the Lord would not have listened; but God has surely listened and heard my voice in prayer. Praise be to God, who has not rejected my prayer or withheld his love from me!* This scripture reinforces what I have been laboring to make clear to you: harboring sin in our lives is a sure way of God not answering our prayers.

Principles in the Bible cannot be ignored. Just like natural laws are binding, spiritual laws or principles are binding too. One of the natural laws we know about is the law of gravity. If you throw anything up, you can be sure it will come down because of the gravitational force. The law cannot just be ignored.

The Bible has many principles. For example, give and it shall be given back to you (Luke 6:38), or if you want to gain your life you will lose it and if you are ready to lose it you will gain it (Matthew 10:39). From the above biblical principles, we can see that if you want to have, you have to give. God demonstrated this principle himself when he gave his only son in order to have us back to himself. People think that the way to have is to hoard more and more only to realize that it does not work that way. Many people do not want to surrender their lives fully to Christ because they fear that they may end up living unfulfilled lives. They end up losing it to drugs, HIV/Aids and other strategies of the enemy of our souls.

I dare say that God is more than willing and ready to answer our prayers more than we expect. The major obstacle is our sins.

Surely the arm of the Lord is not too short to save, nor his ear too dull to hear. But your iniquities have separated you from your God; your sins have hidden his face from you, so that he will not hear. For your hands are stained with blood, your fingers with guilt. Your lips have spoken lies, and your tongue mutters wicked things. ~Isaiah 59:1-3

God has several attributes we know about that make us marvel. Some of His attributes include: He is able, He is merciful, He is good, He is loving, He is caring, He is patient, He is righteous, He is just, He is faithful, He is good.

One of the attributes I like about God is that he is able, meaning that there is nothing that is impossible with our God. You see, some people can give you promises that are totally beyond their means. God is different because there is nothing that is too difficult for him. He can heal us, provide for us, and restore us. There are lots of problems that confront humanity and we wonder how to solve them. Broken families, sour relationships, chronic diseases, poverty, accidents, failures and so forth are some things that humanity has to keep fighting on a daily basis. The solution to these problems has to be prayer from hearts that have been cleansed and forgiven.

The Key

Repentance is key for every believer. Repentance is a radical change of attitude. We must be sorrowful of our sins and this godly sorrow is what works repentance. Many people think that repentance is casual confession of the sin they have committed. If you are not sorry for your sin then you are playing some religious game that is not going to help you.

Most of the things we suffer from are because of sin.

One day as he was teaching, Pharisees and teachers of the law, who had come from every village of Galilee and from Judea and Jerusalem, were sitting there. And the power of the Lord was present for him to heal the sick. Some men came carrying a paralytic on a mat and tried to take him into the house to lay him before Jesus. When they could not find a way to do this because of the crowd, they went up on the roof and lowered him on his mat through the tiles into the middle of the crowd, right in front of Jesus. When Jesus saw their faith, he said, "Friend, your sins are forgiven." The Pharisees and the teachers of the law began thinking to themselves, "Who is this fellow who speaks blasphemy? "Who can forgive sin but God alone?" Jesus knew what they were thinking and asked, "Why are you thinking these things in your hearts? Which is easier: to say, 'Your sins are forgiven,' or to say, 'Get up and walk'? But that you may know that the Son of Man has authority on earth to forgive sins…." He said to the paralyzed man, "I tell you, get up, take your mat and go home." Immediately he stood up in front of them, took what he had been lying on and went home praising God. ~Luke 5:17-25

Jesus knows exactly where the problem is and he wants to deal with it from the roots. Dealing with superficial manifestations of a problem is not a cure.

Sometimes it is very irritating to go to the doctor with a stomach problem and all he does is to ask you to open your mouth. He keeps checking your eyes and other places you think are not relevant to your problem. The doctor knows better and does not want to just deal with symptoms but the exact problem. All that people expected Jesus to do for the paralyzed man was a touch of healing. But Jesus knew better that sin was the problem that needed to be dealt with. After dealing with sin, healing followed.

Genuine Repentance

Genuine repentance is necessary if we are to get answers. Repentance is a radical change of attitude. You have to turn away from your wicked ways. If you have repented and are walking right with God then He will hear your prayers and send you answers. The story of King Hezekiah proves my point:

In those days Hezekiah became ill and was at the point of death. The prophet Isaiah son of Amoz went to him and said, "This is what the Lord says: Put your house in order, because you are going to die; you will not recover." Hezekiah turned his face to the wall and prayed to the Lord, "Remember, O Lord, how I have walked before you faithfully and with wholehearted devotion and have done what is good in your eyes." And Hezekiah wept bitterly. Then the word of the Lord came to Isaiah: "Go and tell Hezekiah, 'This is what the Lord, the God of your father David, says: I have heard your prayer and seen your tears; I will add fifteen years to your life. And I will deliver you and this city from the hand of the King of Assyria. I will defend this city.'" ~Isaiah 38:1-6

Hezekiah was confronted with a very difficult scenario—he was going to die. I wonder what many of us would have done if we were put in Hezekiah's shoes. Most likely many would have pleaded with Isaiah the prophet to intercede on our behalf. The man of God, Hezekiah, knew exactly whom to turn to at the time he faced his greatest crisis. This man had not cherished sin in his life and had served God wholeheartedly. After mentioning the state of his heart, he got fifteen years bonus. I am persuaded that people who do not harbor sin in their lives will always have 'bonuses' when they pray. If your prayer is going to work then you have to be a faithful person who is going to serve God wholeheartedly.

I hope you understand by now that repentance is not a pious collection of words directed to God. We must have godly sorrow of the sins we have committed. Many religious people confess their sins but this is not matched by a change in attitude or deed. When we are repenting, we are telling God that we are sorry for the wrong we have done and that we do not want to do it again.

Our Lord himself went about asking people to repent of their sins as indicated in Mark 1:14-15. *After John was put in prison, Jesus went into Galilee, proclaiming the good news of God. "The time has come," he said. "The kingdom of God is near. Repent and believe the good news!"*

Jesus knew that the only way men could begin a relationship with God is when men realized that they are sinful and willing to ask God to forgive them.

The story of the prodigal son is an amazing account of how a young man came back to his senses and saw the need to repent and ask his father for forgiveness:

When he came to his senses, he said, "How many of my father's hired men have food to spare, and here I am starving to death! I will set out and go back to my father and say to him: Father, I have sinned against heaven and against you. I am no longer worthy to be called your son; make me like one of your hired men". So he got up and went to his father. But while he was still a long way off, his father saw him and was filled with compassion for him; he ran to his son, threw his arms around him and kissed him. The son said to him, "Father, I have sinned against heaven and against you. I am no longer worthy to be called your son." But the father said to his servants, "Quick! Bring the best robe and put it on him. Put a ring on his finger and sandals on his feet." ~ Luke 15:17-22

According to this parable, the father accepted the son back despite the fact that the son had done a wrong thing. All the son needed to do was to go back to the father and ask for forgiveness. If this father was able to accept back his son, how much more will our heavenly Father accept us back if we go back to him in repentance? Like the father in the above parable, our God is waiting to embrace us if only we turn to him.

God is not pleading with us to repent; he is actually commanding us to repent.

In the past God overlooked such ignorance, but now he commands all people everywhere to repent. ~Acts 17:30

Restoration

Over the years, I have learned that many relationships can be restored through repentance. We have to refuse the spirit of pride that stops us from repenting when we are wrong. The antidote for the blame game is repentance.

As prayer warriors, we are not to conceal sin but deal with it through repentance. As we call on God through repentance, we will not have sin residing in us. Repentance leads to restoration, which in turn leads to answered prayers.

I now want to draw your attention to 2 Chronicles 7:13-15; *"When I shut up the heavens so that there is no rain, or command locusts to devour the land or send a plague among my people, if my people, who are called by my name, will humble themselves and pray and seek my face and turn from their wicked ways, then will I hear from heaven and will forgive their sin and will heal their land. Now my eyes will be open and my ears attentive to the prayers offered in this place."*

Some things that we endure like calamities, drought, accidents, diseases and so forth are sometimes consequences of our sins. People need to develop spiritual eyes with which to see things. Think about the things that happen around the globe: homosexuality, abortion, idolatry, corruption, rape, murder, devil worship, injustices, oppressions, racism, adultery, robbery, etc.... Many people claim to be atheists in our days and sins are committed in an unprecedented manner. God is grieved in his heart. In Romans 6:23, *"For the wages of sin is death, but the gift of God is eternal life in Christ Jesus our Lord."*

I am convinced that we are worse than Sodom and Gomorrah. Someone once said that if God does not judge us then he would have to apologize to the people of Sodom and

Gomorrah. Our sins can bring about God's wrath that can be manifested in many ways—hurricanes, earthquakes, famine, war and so on. There are curses that come to a people or nation as a direct result of disobedience.

However, if you do not obey the Lord your God and do not carefully follow all his commands and decrees I am giving you today, all these curses will come upon you and overtake you: You will be cursed in the city and cursed in the country. Your basket and your kneading trough will be cursed. The fruit of your womb will be cursed, and the crops of your land, and the calves of your herds and the lambs of your flocks. You will be cursed when you come in and cursed when you go out. ~Deuteronomy 28:15-19

The rest of the verses in this chapter mention the other curses that will come upon those that have disobeyed God.

Our sins have consequences. But the Bible tells us that if we humble ourselves and ask God to forgive us (repent) then he will pardon our sins and heal our land.

If we claim to be without sin, we deceive ourselves and the truth is not in us. If we confess our sins, he is faithful and just and will forgive us our sins and purify us from all unrighteousness. ~1 John 1:8-9

The answer to the predicament of humanity lies in genuine repentance and turning away from our wicked ways. It is only through these that God can pardon us and begin intervening in our situations.

It is time we acknowledge the fact that no amount of diplomatic talks and technological advancement is going to deliver humanity from the judgments visited upon humanity. It is only through repentance that our sins will be forgiven and God will heal our lands.

Benefits

The benefit of turning from our wicked ways and calling on God is thrilling as shown in 2 Chronicles 7:15, "*Now my eyes will be open and my ears attentive to the prayers offered in this place.*" God will answer the cries of our hearts and meet us at the point of our needs. Look at what will happen to those that are obedient:

If you fully obey the Lord your God and carefully follow his commands I give you today, the Lord your God will set you high above all the nations on earth. All these blessings will come upon you and accompany you if you obey the Lord your God: You will be blessed in the city and blessed in the country. The fruit of your womb will be blessed, and the crops of your land and the young of your livestock—the calves of your herds and the lambs of your flocks. Your basket and your kneading trough will be blessed. You will be blessed when you come in and blessed when you go out. ~Deuteronomy 28:1-6

Believers are the ones who determine whether judgment comes on a nation or whether it is spared from God's wrath depending on whether or not we are praying.

Throughout the pages of scripture, we see God sparing his people because of a few faithful people who stood in the gap. Moses had to stand in the gap when God's wrath was about to hit the Israelites. At one point God was so angry at the Israelites that he threatened to finish them and raise another generation for himself. Moses pleaded with him and he spared the Israelites. Moses was a unique person and the Bible says he was the most humble person on earth. Many people of our days would have told God to go ahead and finish off everybody else and raise a new generation. An intercessor must be a person that values others and that is why Moses qualified as a great intercessor, having been willing to die in the place of the stiff-necked Israelites.

As believers, we are the ones to stand in the gap and repent of the sins of our nations. We know that wickedness is a reproach to a nation but righteousness exalts a nation. As men and women of prayer, we should bring the sins of our people before God and ask him to have mercy and forgive us. There are a lot of curses that are given to the disobedient; it is up to us to stand in the gap on their behalf.

Prayer and Fasting

A story is given in Matthew 17:14-21:

And when they were come to the multitude, there came to him a certain man, kneeling down to him, and saying, Lord, have mercy on my son: for he is a lunatic, and sore vexed: for often he falls into the fire, and often into the water. And I brought him to your disciples, and they could not cure him. Then Jesus answered and said, "O faithless and perverse generation, how long shall I be with you? How long shall I suffer you? Bring him here to me". And Jesus rebuked the devil; and he departed out of him: and the child was cured that very hour. Then came the disciples to Jesus apart, and said, "Why could we not cast him out?" And Jesus said to them, "Because of your unbelief: for verily I say to you, If you have faith as a grain of mustard seed, you shall say to this mountain, remove hence to yonder place; and it shall remove; and nothing shall be impossible for you. However, this kind goes not out but by prayer and fasting". (KJV)

We realize that prayer and fasting is a powerful weapon that believers can use to destroy the works of the enemy. My goal is reaching people of a religion that place a high premium on fasting. Every year, they set apart a number of days to fast. Their kind of fasting is followed like the biblical truth. Should you miss a day of fasting during the designated period of time for whatever reason, you are supposed to compensate! When it is the fasting period, young children that have begun schooling are not spared from the exercise. My friends believe that they have direct access to God during this period of fasting.

We must realize that fasting is not a practice confined to Christian circles only. Other religious groups, including animists, also fast.

The first time I was requested to fast was during my first year in the university. The whole Christian Union was praying and fasting about a mission that we were to have—crusades, door to door sharing and other approaches. All of us were to fast for twenty-four hours without food or drink. I initially wondered how it was going to work since I had never been involved in this kind of exercise before. All fears notwithstanding, I decided to be involved. To be honest with you, the temptation of breaking the fast by 11 am was very strong, but I managed to resist it. I felt like giving up by 3 pm but I survived by some miraculous intervention. I was so hungry and felt extremely weak. That evening, I went to sleep hoping that God would accelerate the speed of the night so I could break my fast early in the morning. That night was terrible because of the great hunger pain that would not allow me to sleep. At 4 am, I found a justification that it was already morning and broke the fast!

Excuses and Obstacles

There are many excuses you can use to stop a fast just like there are excuses for you not to fast. Some of the common excuses I hear include:

1) I do not think I can make it. Prayer and fasting is meant for the spiritual giants and I am not one of them.
2) My health situation does not allow me to fast—I might die in the process.
3) You know, I have to be wise and avoid these extreme practices.
4) I have so much work to do and it would be impossible for me to fast under these circumstances.
5) My hotel bill has been paid for and I would be a bad steward if I do not eat meals that have been paid for.
6) I do not have a specific reason as to why I am to fast. It would be boring, being hungry without words to tell God.
7) Everything is working fine for me and I do not see why I should punish my body.

The list is endless. The excuses may look good and convincing but they are there to deny you opportunity to experience God through this practice of denial.

The enemy will always try to stop you from prayer and fasting by bringing excuses your way. It will take a man and a woman who know that we are in a war to succeed in dismissing those excuses.

I have found out that it is often during my time of prayer and fasting that very unlikely fellows invite me for lunch, a drink or supper. I wonder where they are when I am open to such invitations.

For reasons I do not know, it seems every time that I set myself for a long period of prayer and fasting that I am invited to a good hotel for meetings that will last a week. Usually, the bills are paid for and I can avail myself and enjoy the delicacies. I remember one incident when I was attending a weeklong meeting in Nairobi. I had been booked into an expensive guesthouse. The pressure was so much upon me to eat because my meals had been paid for already. I struggled in my mind with the issue and nearly justified why I should eat. Then a strong conviction came within me that made me resilient and I decided that my faithfulness to the commitment I had made was not going to be compromised in any way.

One thing that is sure from my experiences is that every time that I have defied the voices persuading me to give up praying and fasting, I encountered God and he did a work that remains to the date.

It is during my time of praying and fasting that God has revealed to me which way to go at a crossroad. I can attest to the fact that I would not be where I am today had it not been for my life of prayer and fasting.

Fasting for a Ministry

Our own Lord and Savior Jesus Christ began his ministry after forty days of prayer and fasting.

Jesus, full of the Holy Spirit, returned from the Jordan and was led by the Spirit in the desert, where for forty days he was tempted by the devil. He ate nothing during those days, and at the end of them he was hungry. The devil said to him, "If you are the Son of God, tell this stone to become bread." Jesus answered, "It is written: 'Man does not live on bread alone'." ~ Luke 4:1-4

If Jesus, who is the Son of God, fasted then we need to fast all the more. We know that Jesus was 100% God and 100% man. He faced all the challenges that we face when fasting and yet he did it.

In essence, when fasting we are telling God that we love him more than food or anything else that our bodies might want. We are telling him that we are desperate for his presence more than anything else. He is our first priority and other things are secondary. Fasting brings you to a point of surrender to the will of the master.

Jesus prayed and fasted and the result was amazing things happened in his ministry that caused the world to marvel: the eyes of the blind seeing, the ears of the deaf being unblocked, the crippled walking, the lepers being cleansed, the mad being made whole, the epileptic being healed, the dead being raised back to life, the demon possessed being delivered, the hungry being fed, sicknesses and diseases of all kinds being healed. It is amazing the kind of things God can accomplish through us if we are men and women of prayer and fasting.

Prayer and fasting humbles you and you learn to decrease so that Christ may increase in you. We are aware that things happen not by might nor by power but by the Spirit of God. Prayer and fasting will reinforce this truth in you. Many believers reach a point in their lives when they begin to rely on the experiences and even begin to think that they are indispensable. If you are a guitarist, you miss Sunday service so they can feel your absence and appreciate your importance. If you are a pastor, you do not even seek God concerning the message to deliver because it is all in your mind. Pride begins to creep in. The antidote to the above is to go before the master in prayer and fasting. Just like I shared about how weak I felt the first time I fasted, you will feel weak and begin yearning for God's strength—not your own. God likes to use weak people to confound those that are strong. If we do not pray and fast, we begin to feel like we are the ones who are in charge and in the extreme begin to brag how God is using us. Before long, you will find yourself taking the glory that belongs to God because of the pride in you. Remember that God does not share his glory with anyone.

Show me a man who is mightily being used by God and I will show you a person who has cultivated the discipline of prayer and fasting.

The Bible commands us to humble ourselves under the mighty hand of God and we will be exalted (James 4:10). One way to humble ourselves is through prayer and fasting.

Fasting in a Crisis

A number of times in the Bible, we see people confronted with terrible situations in which they resort to prayer and fasting; they all invariably see God's hand of deliverance.

Take a look at the book of Esther and you find the Jews under the threat of annihilation. The mastermind of this scheme is none other than Haman: the very man King Xerxes had elevated, giving him a seat of honor higher than that of all the other nobles. Mordecai was the source of the trouble for the Jews because he refused to comply with the practice of kneeling down and paying honor whenever Haman passed by. Haman devised a strategy that saw him being given the signet ring from the king's finger and the fate of the Jews was sealed. They were to be totally annihilated. But something happened. *Then Esther sent this reply to Mordecai: "Go, gather together all the Jews who are in Susa, and fast for me. Do not eat or drink for three days, night or day. I and my maids will fast as you do. When this is done, I will go to the king, even though it is against the law. And if I perish, I perish." So Mordecai went away and carried out all of Esther's instructions.* ~Esther 4:15-17

It is important to remember here that the Jews faced a terrible situation as the dispatches had already been sent by couriers to all the king's provinces with the order to destroy, kill and annihilate all the Jews—young and old, women and little children on a single day, the thirteenth day of the twelfth month. Having prayed and fasted, Esther did what was against the law and went to the king. Under normal circumstances, Esther should have to die. See the way God came to her aid:

On *the third day Esther put on her royal robes and stood in the inner court of the palace, in front of the king's hall. The king was sitting on his royal throne in the hall, facing the entrance. When he saw Queen Esther standing in the court, he was pleased with her and held out to her the gold scepter that was in his hand. So Esther approached and touched the tip of the scepter. Then the king asked, "What is it, Queen Esther? What is your request? Even up to half the kingdom, it will be given you."* ~Esther 5:1-3

Wow! Prayer and fasting turned a terrible situation into a favorable one. Now it is not death waiting but a reward of up to half the kingdom!

People have changed their fate by calling on God through prayer and fasting. Families have been delivered from curses as God's children called on him through prayer and fasting. Churches and ministries have impacted the world significantly as they prayed and fasted. Countries have seen their GDP (gross domestic product) go up as God's children pray and fast for these countries. Wives have prayed and fasted for the salvation of their husbands and have seen it come to pass. Parents have prayed and fasted for their children to be delivered from drug addictions and have seen it happen. Couples without children have prayed and fasted for God to give them children and God made it come true so that they have touched their babies with their own hands. Marriages have been restored as people prayed and fasted. Relationships have been restored as people who saw themselves as enemies committed the issues before God through prayer and fasting. People have come out of the bondage of poverty as they called on God through prayer and fasting. I have no space to record what I have seen happen as God's children prayed and fasted for the Master to come through for them.

The Bible makes it clear that God will not despise a broken and a contrite heart (Psalm 51:17).

It is surprising to see how the fortune of Haman changed after the Jews prayed and fasted:

So the king and Haman went to dine with Queen Esther, and as they were drinking wine on that second day, the king again asked, "Queen Esther, what is your petition? It will be given you. What is your request? Even up to half the kingdom, it will be granted." Then Queen Esther answered, "If I have found favor with you, O king, and if it pleases your majesty, grant me my life---this is my petition. And spare my people---this is my request. For I and my people have been sold for destruction and slaughter and annihilation. If we had merely been sold as male and female slaves, I would have kept quiet, because no such distress would justify disturbing the king." King Xerxes asked Queen Esther, "Who is he? Where is the man who has dared to do such a thing?" Esther said, "The adversary and enemy is this vile Haman." Then

Haman was terrified before the king and queen. The king got up in a rage, left his wine and went out into the palace garden. But Haman, realizing that the king had already decided his fate, stayed behind to beg Queen Esther for his life. Just as the king returned from the palace garden to the banquet hall, Haman was falling on the couch where Esther was reclining. The king exclaimed, "Will he even molest the queen while she is with me in the house?" ~ Esther 7:1-8

From that moment, things started working against Haman and eventually he was hanged on the very gallows he had prepared for Mordecai. You want your situations and those of your friends changed? Try calling on God through prayer and fasting.

Fasting for a Nation

I believe God is looking for watchmen who are going to stand in the gap on behalf of their nations. These are people who are going to pray and fast until the kingdom of God is established in their nations.

I have posted watchmen on your walls, O Jerusalem; they will never be silent day or night. You who call on the Lord, give yourselves no rest, and give him no rest till he establishes Jerusalem and makes her the praise of the earth. ~Isaiah 62:6-7

I personally believe that there are countries that have been spared from civil strife and even genocide because of people praying and fasting on their behalf. One such country is Kenya. Many countries surrounding Kenya have gone through tough moments. Somalia on the east has been without a government for almost a decade and a half. The government of Siad Barre was toppled, and for quite some time the militiamen had been controlling different parts of the country. A new government has been formed although it is still trying to find its niche. The country has not known peace for many years and most of its people are scattered all over the world. Many Somalis are now refugees in both Dadaab refugee camp and Kakuma refugee camp in Kenya.

On the west of Kenya is Uganda. Uganda lost many lives during the leadership of dictator Idi Amin. The Lord's Resistance Army of Joseph Kony has terrorized northern Uganda for almost two decades now. People live in great fear in such towns as Gulu.

On the northern side of Kenya is Ethiopia and Sudan. Ethiopians suffered under the regime of Mengistu and many people who did not share in his ideologies were tortured and imprisoned. Many Ethiopians ran away to become refugees and some sought asylum in foreign countries. The war between Ethiopia and Eritrea (which was once a province of Ethiopia) is still very fresh in our minds—many lives were lost in the process. The tension is still very high between these two countries over disputed boundary lines.

The Khartoum government (dominated by Arab Muslims) has been fighting with Southern Sudanese (Africans—Christians and animist) for over two decades until recently when they signed a comprehensive peace agreement that has seen the southerners being co-opted in the Khartoum government. Many lives were lost during the war and millions displaced from their homes. Many Sudanese are still in refugee camps in Kenya, Uganda, and Ethiopia. The war in Darfur is still a puzzle as the Arab militiamen continue to attack Africans in the western part of Sudan. Many people have died and been displaced from their homes.

I cannot stop before mentioning one of the worst genocides to ever have happened. Rwandans turned against one another; the Hutu's and the Tutsi's killed one another to such an extent that nearly eight hundred thousand people are estimated to have died. This country is one of Kenya's neighboring countries.

While terrible things were happening in its neighborhood, Kenya remained intact. This does not mean that Kenyans have been more righteous than their neighbors. The only thing you must know is that Kenya has had many intercessory teams praying for the country.

In the Kenyan election of 2002, prophets of doom predicted that it was going to be a bloody election. What these people did not know was that many believers were praying and fasting for the country. Twenty-four hour prayer chains were going on in different towns in the country. Overnight prayer meetings for the country were a common phenomenon prior to and during the campaigns.

I remember I was in Uganda during the entire period of the campaign and it was amazing to see our friends, Dr. Robert Mwadime and his wife Sonia, mobilize Kenyans in Kampala for a special time of praying for Kenya. Kampala Pentecostal Church

South set apart a Sunday service to pray for the Kenyan election. I was delighted to have participated in this event. Believers prayed and fasted, asking God for a peaceful election. Apparently, many believers knew who the choice was and so come election, Mwai Kibaki won the election with overwhelming votes. The peaceful hand over by former president Daniel arap Moi was a result of God's intervention after believers prayed and fasted. It is sad that African leaders hardly hand over power unless coerced by the power of a gun but true prayer and fasting directed to God is changing all that.

When France was going through rebellion, England was experiencing great revivals because of people like John Wesley, George Whitefield, and Charles Wesley. These men were known for their discipline of prayer and fasting. Prayer and fasting can move countries from civil strife to revival which results in prosperity of a nation.

Fasting for a City

When believers fast and pray for a city, God answers with His mercy. Let's prove this point by looking at Jonah 1:1-2, *The word of the Lord came to Jonah son of Amittai: "Go to the great city of Nineveh and preach against it, because its wickedness has come up before me."*

This city deserved God's punishment but God wanted it to have a chance to repent. Initially, Jonah refused but having been swallowed by a fish, he accepted to go and proclaim the word of the Lord. When the people heard that Nineveh was not going to be there any more after forty days because of their wickedness, they declared a fast, from the greatest to the least and they put on sackcloth.

When the news reached the king of Nineveh, he rose from his throne, took off his royal robes, covered himself with sackcloth and sat down in the dust. Then he issued a proclamation in Nineveh: "By the decree of the king and his nobles: Do not let any man or beast, herd or flock, taste anything; do not let them eat or drink. But let man and beast be covered with sackcloth. Let everyone call urgently on God. Let them give up their evil ways and their violence. Who knows? God may yet relent and with compassion turn from his fierce anger so that we will not perish." When God saw what they did and how they turned from their evil ways, he had compassion and did not bring upon them the destruction he had threatened. ~Jonah 3:6-10

I hope you can see what humbling themselves through prayer and fasting had done! The city of Nineveh was spared because they became remorseful of their sins and asked for God's mercy and forgiveness.

There are nations that have become so wicked and face God's wrath unless God's children will stand in the gap on their behalf and ask him for mercy. From the above scripture, even children and beasts were not spared from the fast. It is time that believers introduce their children to the practice of prayer and fasting. For a start, it does not have to be a dry fast for twenty-four hours. They might just skip breakfast or four o'clock tea. With time, they will begin to grow in this discipline. We have to share with our children the importance of prayer and fasting and leave them to make their own decisions. We must never coerce them because this will just drive them away. One thing to note is that our children have to be believers before we can share with them about prayer and fasting.

Ideas for Fasting

We have to realize that prayer and fasting is totally different from starving ourselves or going on a hunger strike. I know there are people that have gone on hunger strikes for a number of days because of various reasons—to be released from prison or for some demand to be met. Many people, especially ladies, are known to starve themselves so they can reduce their weight or maintain a desirable weight. There is a marked difference between starvation, hunger strikes and fasting. In fasting, you are humbling yourself before God and asking for his intervention concerning issues that you are facing. It is of paramount importance that you spend quality time in the word of God during your prayer and fasting time. Fasting can be tedious and wearisome if we do not interact with the word of God. If you are to pray according to the will of God then you must know the word of God. Therefore, we need to study the Bible.

Your time of prayer and fasting will be maximized if you develop a program to guide you on that day. Reading and meditating on God's word should take a good proportion of your time of prayer and fasting.

We all have interests and desires that are contrary to the will of God for our lives. It is the word of God that straightens up those interests and desires.

Prayer and fasting is also about listening to God. We are so used to talking that listening is a problem. One major cause of divorce in our times is poor communication. When one is talking, the other is not listening but preparing in his mind what to say next. We have taken our 'talking syndrome' to God, pouring out to him everything that can be said and then dashing off without giving him our ears. Prayer and fasting should offer us the opportunity to listen to our Master. Only a word from the Master can change your situation for better.

The glory of a man is in searching the secrets of God and the glory of God is in concealing those secrets (Proverbs 25:2). True seekers especially those who pray and fast find such secrets.

Another great idea of how to maximize your time of prayer and fasting is to identify a particular portion of scripture and then pray it back to God. One good thing about this strategy is that you can be sure you are praying according to the will of God. When the devil tempted Jesus during his forty days of prayer and fasting, he responded by saying 'It is written'. What is written is more important than the words that we may say. Jesus knew what was written and used it to defeat the enemy. We, too, have the privilege of knowing what is written so that when the enemy comes, we will be able to point out what is written.

Abusing the Fast

Much as prayer and fasting is very important in the lives of believers, it is also true that others abuse it for their own selfish reasons. The hypocrites do not fast for the right reason. The Bible tells us not to be like hypocrites.

When you fast, do not look somber as the hypocrites do, for they disfigure their faces to show men they are fasting. I tell you the truth, they have received their reward in full. But when you fast, put oil on your head and wash your face, so that it will not be obvious to men that you are fasting, but only to your Father, who is unseen; and your Father, who sees what is done in secret, will reward you. ~Matthew 6:16-18

The hypocrites were fasting for the wrong reasons—to get glory from men. They wanted to be sure that the whole world saw that they were fasting. They actually wanted to be seen as more spiritual than the rest of the people. They even went as far as disfiguring their faces so everybody would realize that they were fasting.

The Bible tells us that those who fast so they can be seen should not expect any reward from God since they already have the glory from men. It is up to you to decide whether you want appreciation and recognition from men or an answer from the Lord.

In our days, we hear people talk about how often they pray and fast. Some have good intentions and motives for sharing their prayer and fasting lives, others just want recognition from men. Be different by adopting Jesus' principle—wash yourself, put oil on your face and put a big smile on your face. I must point out at this time that it is wrong to think that fasting will automatically make you gain a hearing from God. The Israelites were victims of this fallacy:

'Why have we fasted', they say, 'and you have not seen it? Why have we humbled ourselves, and you have not noticed?' Yet on the day of your fasting, you do as you please and exploit all your workers. Your fasting ends in quarreling and strife, and in striking each other with wicked fists. You cannot fast as you do today and expect your voice to be heard on high. ~Isaiah 58:3-4

Isaiah told the Israelites that God could not honor a fast that is not based on genuine conduct. We cannot engage in wickedness and expect that our fasting is going to cancel out our sins. These same people that were fasting were the very ones that were exploiting their workers, quarrelling and striking each other.

If we are to experience a breakthrough in our fasting, then we must deal with sins in our lives by confessing them and by turning away from every wickedness.

If we confess our sins, he is faithful and just and will forgive us our sins and purify us from all unrighteousness. ~1 John 1:9

Fasting For Guidance

The Bible tells of many people that prayed and fasted for God's intervention in their situation or just to hear from him for guidance. One such person is Moses.

Moses was there with the Lord forty days and forty nights without eating bread or drinking water. And he wrote on the tablets the words of the covenant—the Ten Commandments. ~Exodus 34:28

David also prayed and fasted for the healing of the son he bore with Bathsheba.

After Nathan had gone home, the Lord struck the child that Uriah's wife had borne to David, and he became ill. David pleaded with God for the child. He fasted and went into his house and spent the nights lying on the ground. ~2 Samuel 12:15-16

Several kings in the Bible also directed the people to pray and fast whenever the prophets had warned of the impending wrath of God. Whenever they were genuine, God always forgave their sins.

As earlier indicated, prayer and fasting is not just confined to Christianity. All major religions in the world practice prayer and fasting although with different motives. Muslims fast to get Allah's blessings, to have self-control and to purify body and spirit. Buddhists fast to guard, control and lift the senses to a peak experience.

Over the centuries, we have heard of people who fasted for reasons other than truly seeking God's face. Mohandas Gandhi used fasting as penance and as a means of political protest. According to him, one could not pray without fasting or fast without praying. Philosophers Plato and Socrates recommended fasting for increasing mental and physical effectiveness.

In Christian circles, good examples of men of God who modeled fasting include:

1. John Wesley (1703-1791): He was a member of the Holy club of Oxford that fasted each Wednesday and Friday. Wesley refused to ordain a man into the Methodist ministry who would not fast until 4 p.m. every Wednesday and Friday.

2. Jonathan Edwards (1703-1758): He led the 'Great Awakening' in New England. It is said that he fasted three days before the revival in which he preached the famous sermon 'Sinners in the hand of an angry God'. When Edwards rose from praying to preach, his countenance reflected God's presence.

3. George Finney (1792-1875): It is said that he prayed and fasted every time he felt devoid of God's power.

4. Andrew Murray (1828-1917): According to him, fasting validates our claim to sacrifice anything for our request on behalf of the kingdom of God.

5. Girolamo Savonarola (1452-1498): After fasting, he became so weak that somebody had to support him in the pulpit. His audience wept, while beating their breast and crying for God's mercy. The streets of Florence, Italy were silent because of his sermon that caused fear and remorse of sin.

6. Charles. H. Spurgeon (1834-1892): He is credited with the statement "our seasons of fasting and prayer at the tabernacle have been high days indeed. Never has heaven's gate stood wider. Never has our hearts been nearer the central glory."

The people above and many more brought revivals in their nations and the impact was felt all over the world. I hope that you have seen how the practice of prayer and fasting is important from a biblical point of view. Prayer and fasting is just as important and relevant in our days as it was in the past. I pray that you are going to be willing to deny yourself food, drinks and other things that your body values for a time so that you can meet with God.

Prayer and Praise/Worship

Praise has something to do with what God does. In other words, when praising God we adore the glory of his power. Worship on the other hand seeks to adore the person of God—who he is to us.

God has attributes that should cause us to be on our knees to worship him. Some of his attributes include: He is faithful, He is loving, He is perfect, He is eternal, He is majestic, He is awesome, He is the truth, He is compassionate, He is caring, He is righteous, He is just, He is merciful, He is gracious, He is mighty. The list is endless.

Worship is broader than we think and is meant to quicken our conscience to God's holiness and to purify our imaginations by God's beauty. Worship helps our hearts to open up for the entrance of God's truth. God's truth will in turn set us free indeed. Many people are in terrible predicaments because they have not yet known God's truth. Through worship, God tells us his mind about how to go about issues and before long we will come out of the quagmire we find ourselves in.

People find themselves feeding their minds with dirty things. These same things lead us to worry, fear, hopelessness, and doubt. If you are a worshipper, your mind will be purified from all these. Instead of being fearful you will be courageous, instead of being hopeless you will be full of hope, instead of doubting you will have faith. In other words you will believe God and his word regardless of how bad your situation is.

Praising God is something that every believer should practice doing all the time and not just during the Sunday service.

Psalm 150: *Praise the Lord. Praise God in his sanctuary; praise him in his mighty heavens. Praise him for his acts of power; praise him for his surpassing greatness. Praise him with the sounding of the trumpet, praise him with the harp and lyre, praise him with tambourine and dancing, praise him with the strings and flute, praise him with the clash of cymbals, praise him with the resounding cymbals. Let everything that has breath praise the Lord. Praise the Lord.*

I know that many choirs in Kenya have been formed with the intention of singing songs that praise the leader. The leaders always get excited hearing such songs directed to them and they find themselves rewarding heavily those choirs. If we can praise our leaders, how much more ought we to praise our maker? As God's children, we have to know that praising God is something that we should be doing all the time.

Psalm 30:4: *Sing to the Lord, you saints of his; praise his holy name.*

There are many ways of praising God that include dancing, singing, and using instruments such as flutes, cymbals, guitars, pianos, etc....

I remember as a young child, whenever I wanted something from dad I would make sure that the environment was good before I could share about what I wanted. A bad environment will guarantee a 'No' answer when it ought to have been a 'YES'. In order to have a good environment, I used stories as icebreakers. In the end I ended up getting what I needed. Many people do not know how to present themselves before the throne of God—we just appear and begin mentioning our shopping list. Our Father must be wondering what kind of people we are. God is interested in meeting your need but he is more interested in having fellowship with you.

Praise/Worship Brings Victory

Praise and worship prepares you as you appear before the throne of grace. Remember that your conscience is quickened by God's holiness and his beauty purifies your imagination. Praise and worship are powerful tools that God uses to grant believers victory over their enemies.

In Joshua Chapter 6, we are told of how Joshua instructed the Israelites to march around Jericho once a day for six days. On the seventh day, they were to march around Jericho seven times. Look at what happened after the people had gone around Jericho the seventh time. In verse 16: *The seventh time around, when the priests sounded the trumpet blast, Joshua commanded the people, "Shout! For the Lord has given you the city!"* Verse 20: *When the trumpets sounded, the people shouted, and at the sound of the trumpet, when the people gave a loud shout, the wall collapsed: so every man charged straight in, and they took the city.*

I assume that you know that Jericho was tightly shut up. When God's people started praising with trumpets and loud shouts, the wall collapsed!

The Bible makes it clear that God inhabits the praises of his people (Psalms 22:3). David seems to have understood this truth very well. When God gave him victory in a battle he danced for the Lord so aggressively that one of his wives took offence in it. To David, praising God was more important than the title of a king. The tragedy of our time is that some people think they are too important to praise God. They look upon dancing and shouting to the Lord as something shameful. Thank God that there are people who are reversing this thinking. One such group is the "Promise Keepers". It is amazing to see this group drawing huge crowds of men together in different cities with the single objective of praising and worshipping God! This kind of movement is needed in every part of the globe.

Altars of Praise/Worship

It is time to build altars of praise everywhere so all people would know that God is mighty and deserves praise and worship.

Worship is the sole reason for which God created us. If there is anything like God having a need then it must be the need to be worshipped. God derives pleasure from being worshipped and man derives pleasure from worshipping God.

God is not just looking for any kind of worship but the kind that comes from those who worship in spirit and in truth. I believe that the only work we will do in heaven is that of worship. I challenge you to start worshipping now.

Unfortunately for our generation, worship has been given a very narrow definition as to limit it to slow songs that precede prayer. Worship is broader than that. There are very many ways to worship God. We worship him with our tithes and offerings, we worship him by preaching his word, we worship him by singing to him, we worship him by witnessing to others, we worship him by striving for justice, we worship him by helping the orphans and the widows, we worship him when we obey what he tells us. Students in school know that performing well in their academics is a way of worshipping God.

Somebody said that without worship we shrink and that is the brutal truth. In other words, we are not whole if we are not worshipping our God.

Each of the four living creatures had six wings and was covered with eyes all around, even under his wings. Day and night they never stop saying: "Holy, holy, holy is the Lord God Almighty, who was, and is, and is to come." Whenever the living creatures give glory, honor and thanks to him who sits on the throne and who lives for ever and ever, the twenty-four elders fall down before him who sits on the throne, and worship him who lives for ever and ever. They lay their crowns before the throne and say: "You are worthy, our Lord and God, to receive glory and honor and power, for you created all things, and by your will they were created and have their being." ~Revelation 4:8-11

This portion of scripture is a graphic example of what worship is all about. The work of the twenty-four elders and the living creatures is to worship the king.

As I said earlier, God derives pleasure from being worshipped and men derive pleasure from worshipping God. Man will not be fully satisfied in anything unless what he is doing is done as worship to the master. We have to know that sports, business and whatever we do can be done as a way of worshipping God. An athlete who won gold in the Olympic games once said that when he runs, he runs really fast and that to him it is a way of worshipping God. I submit to you that we desperately need this attitude back in the church because it is the right perspective about worship. The dichotomy of the secular and the spiritual has done great damage. Spiritual issues have been left for Sunday service and sometimes mid-week service for those who have them. According to this line of thinking, what we do in our work place or business is purely secular. This approach to issues needs to be reversed totally so that we understand that what happens in our business and work places is just as spiritual as what takes place in a Sunday service. People should stop thinking that in order for worship to take place there must be guitars, drums, and microphones. These instruments improve the quality of worship to our God but we can easily worship without them.

Housewives need to turn the kitchen into a worship arena as they interact with plates, mugs, spoons, forks, and dishes. Watchmen have a great opportunity of having overnight prayers as they guard. CEO's need to see opportunities of worship as they give speeches in the many seminars and conferences they have. Things would be very different if we made our work and business as spiritual as being in a church.

I encourage you to cultivate the habit of praising God everywhere you are. Praising God does not mean that you must shout loud all the time—sometimes the environment will not allow this and you've got to know how best to worship him wherever you are.

I was recently giving training in a refugee camp that has many nationalities and encouraged them to praise God even in their difficult situations. Praising God can bring solutions to what has bothered us so much. I know many people that spend most of their time binding the devil at the expense of praising God. I reminded the refugees that there are things to be bound, things to be resisted and things to run away from. Joseph needed to run away from Potiphar's wife. The time for binding was over. These refugees learned that they needed to praise God if for nothing else than God sparing their lives when turmoil reigned all around them.

Problem Solving Praise/Worship

We have a tendency to focus on our problem and this sometimes denies us the opportunity to praise God. Every time that I have chosen not to focus on my problems and chose to praise God instead, I have experienced God's hand of deliverance. The truth is that it is not easy to praise God when things are difficult but it is still the best thing to do.

Prayer warriors must put aside complaints and murmurings and clothe themselves with garments of praise.

In Acts 16, God is mightily using Paul and Silas when suddenly the owners of the slave girl whom Paul and Silas had prayed for deliverance mobilized people to attack Paul and Silas. Paul and Silas had every reason to complain and murmur but look at what happened:

About midnight Paul and Silas were praying and singing hymns to God, and the other prisoners were listening to them. Suddenly there was such a violent earthquake that the foundations of the prison were shaken. At once all the prison doors flew open, and everybody's chains came loose. The jailer woke up, and when he saw the prison doors open, he drew his sword and was about to kill himself because he thought the prisoners had escaped. But Paul shouted, "Don't harm yourself! We are all here!" ~Acts 16:25-28

Praising God caused the prison doors to fly open. Are you under attack of some kind? Are you feeling like you have lost it all? Try praising God and you will see him at work.

I am glad that God accepts our praises even if they are off-tune — I am not a good singer by any standard (humanly speaking). I remember as a young lad at Tinderet primary school we practiced two songs that we were to present during our music festival. Our school did very well in both of those songs and we qualified for a national competition that was to be held in Nairobi. Every one of us was excited that we were finally going to go to Nairobi. In those days, Nairobi was the preserve of great people. Your value in the village would go up just by visiting 'the city in the sun', as it was known then. Unfortunately for our choir, our number was more than what was required — we were seventy in all. There was a need to reduce our number by five people and so all of us were called to line up so a process of elimination could begin. The criteria they used was to ask somebody to sing a line and on this basis that would determine who was not fit for this important trip. Guess who was the first casualty in this exercise? For some reason, my voice cannot just rhyme with the rest. I am the type that can not fit into a bass, soprano, tenor, alto; I am in-between but not quite sure where. I was extremely disappointed by what befell me that day and concluded that I was not cut out for singing. After receiving Christ, I came to realize that God loves me, and that includes the way I sing. My attitude about singing has changed. I can assure you that I love making a joyful noise to the Lord and more so when I am alone!

The heart from which praise comes is more important to God than how the music sounds. I am not trying to justify off-tune songs. I believe God loves music that is well organized and sung properly.

The priests took their positions, as did the Levites with the Lord's musical instruments, which King David had made for praising the Lord and which were used when he gave thanks, saying, "His love endures forever." Opposite the Levites, the priests blew their trumpets, and all the Israelites were standing. ~2 Chronicles 7:6

Excellent Praise/Worship

God was worshipped in a certain way. Therefore, it is very important for those who lead God's people in praise to strive for excellence so that we give God our best.

I actually appreciate those churches that have invested heavily in instruments with the intention of improving the quality of praise and worship. I know some people become critical when they see churches buying expensive instruments but they ought to know that these instruments are meant to glorify God and not fellow men. If we do not have instruments, we can still go ahead and give him clap offerings and dancing.

At no time should we complain that praise and worship is boring because it is not meant to entertain us but to glorify God. We have a tendency to judge things based on our feelings, but remember that even though our feelings are important, they are not supposed to lead or direct you.

Presence and Power in Praise/Worship

Praise and worship brings the presence of God and his power. His power brings about healing, deliverance, restoration and blessings.

I remember attending an overnight prayer meeting in Uganda in 2002 at Nelson Mandela stadium. The meeting was organized by Pastor Robert Kayanja of Miracle Cathedral (one of the biggest churches in Uganda) together with other pastors in Kampala. Getting into the stadium was a big problem because there were too many people attending the meeting. Vehicles heading to the venue of the meeting were so many that there was a serious traffic problem in the whole city of Kampala. People are so hungry for God in this small East African country. Amongst those attending the overnight prayer meeting was Ugandan First Lady Janet Museveni. Quite a number of ministers and other dignitaries also attended the meeting. Alvin Slaughter led us in praise and worship. There were other singers from Kenya also.

One unique thing about this meeting is that as people were busy praising and worshipping God, miracles began to happen in every corner of the stadium. The presence of God was in the stadium and people did not need pastors or evangelists to lay hands on them—God was doing that himself. Suddenly from nowhere, doves started flying and behaved as if they were dancing in the stadium. The amazing thing is that these doves confined themselves within the stadium as they 'joyfully danced' around. Many of us were stunned at this. I do not want to seem super spiritual, but many associate the dove with the Holy Spirit.

When all the people were being baptized, Jesus was baptized too. And as he was praying, heaven was opened and the Holy Spirit descended on him in bodily form like a dove. And a voice came from heaven: "You are my Son, whom I love; with you I am well pleased." ~ Luke 3:21-22

I believe God wants to see what happened in Kampala replicated all over the world. We do not need international preachers to lay their hands on us so we can receive healing. We just need to praise and worship Him and leave the rest to God. When God shows up, all your shackles and chains will break.

Praising and worshipping God is a choice that you have to keep making. There are many forces that will seek to make you angry, lazy, bitter, hateful, and ungrateful so that you will not want to praise and worship God. You must initiate spiritual warfare against these forces of hell that would come to rob praise from you.

Finally, be strong in the Lord and in his mighty power. Put on the full armor of God so that you can take your stand against the devil's schemes. For our struggle is not against flesh and blood, but against the rulers, against the authorities, against the powers of this dark world and against the spiritual forces of evil in the heavenly realms. ~Ephesians 6:10-12

Thank God that even though the powers of darkness are against us, we are more than conquerors through Christ who strengthens us (Romans 8:37).

Let me show you the power of praise as shown in 1 Samuel 16:23. *Whenever the spirit from God came upon Saul, David would take his harp and play. Then relief would come to Saul; he would feel better, and the evil spirit would leave him.*

Whenever you feel you are under oppression, refuse the spirit of heaviness and clothe yourself with praise even if things are tough.

Hindering Praise/Worship

There are things that will hinder you from being the vessel of praise that you ought to be. Watching pornographic pictures will pollute your mind and obstruct you from seeing the great works of God and his attributes. Some of these pictures can be seen just once but can take more than a decade to erase from the mind. Our world is full of pornography and you do not have to look for it. It will look for you. We see pornographic pictures displayed by magazine merchants. Sometimes they are gazing at us from big billboards in our cities. You open the Internet and they keep popping up without your permission if you are not protected from them. Young people are in great danger of pornography as there is strong peer pressure to have 'a glance' at a dirty site just once. Trying it once can lead to an addiction that is hard to come out of unless God intervenes with his hand of deliverance.

As people of praise and true worshippers, we must be very deliberate and intentional to avoid watching things that are devised by the enemy to hook us into sin. People do not always fall into sin—it is usually a gradual process.

The picture we see gives us an idea, the idea grows and becomes your word, when the word matures it becomes action, action shapes our attitude, our attitude forms our habit and finally our habit determines our character and final destiny—whether we are going to live with God forever or whether we are going to be eternally separated from him. This is why the Bible tells us to guard our hearts against evil.

As a man or a woman of praise, come up with practical resolutions on how you are going to keep yourself away from pornography. One of your resolutions could be that of protecting your computer from 'the uninvited guests'. Another could be that of spending more of your time digging into the word of God and reading Christian books as opposed to reading secular materials with tendencies toward pornography.

Watching too much television will also feed your mind with things that will only succeed in killing praise and worship in your life. As I am writing this book, Kenya has just gone through the first referendum since it received its independence over forty years ago. There has been clamor for constitutional change in the country for almost fifteen years. The people were given the choice of whether they wanted the proposed new constitution or not. One bad thing about this referendum is that even believers involved themselves in hate campaigns against the opposing side. They spent most of their time watching television on how politicians were busy abusing each other and thought they were immune from such talks. Before long they started talking dirty just like the politicians. All of us are weak vessels and we have as much potential to sin as the 'sinners'. We need to be wise and not expose ourselves to sin so much.

It is prudent for me to now strike a balance concerning the television issue. I know a church in Kenya that has banned their members from watching television. In fact, they call it a 'one-eyed devil'. I personally believe that we can use television positively—watching informative programs, preaching, gospel music and documentaries. What I am against is the idea of 'feeding' on every dirty thing being shown. In other words, I am advocating for watching television selectively. We also ought to know what our children are watching and offer them advice accordingly. It is true that watching television can be so addictive that it becomes a priority to some people.

Look at what happened during the 2002 World Cup final in Japan and South Korea and you will see how addictive television can be. Church attendance was so low in many Kenyan churches every time Senegal played against any team. Kenyans were aggressively supporting Senegal—the only African country that had hopes of succeeding to the finals. Believers chose to watch twenty-two men running after that thing made of a skin at the expense of gathering together to worship the King of Kings.

I personally was a great footballer that would have easily made it to the national level if I had wanted to. What worries me is the addiction of this game and the way we have a wrong priority in life on how to spend our time. I never cease to wonder what would happen to many believers if Jesus chose to come back during the world cup matches. I hope you understand that I have not said that the game is bad but that we have to maintain a heart of praise and worship even during big events.

Would you go ahead and identify which programs you want to be watching, and for how long? Make sure that you do not spend a lot of your time watching television unless it is something that enables you to see the exalted view of God so you can worship him.

It is time that we build altars of praise everywhere in our work place and everywhere we find ourselves. I challenge those that are influencers in their country to consider pushing for the idea of having a single day every year when people from different towns or villages can gather together at strategic locations with the sole motive of praising and worshipping God. It is hard to imagine what God would do in such gatherings as we forget our denominational differences in order to honor the Lords of Lords.

One thing that has divided churches is the way 'praise and worship' songs are done. Some like singing using hymn books while others like it 'hot'—jumping and clapping really hard for the Lord. Well, I believe we have spent our precious time majoring on the minors. We ought to know that God enjoys diversity. He loves a naked dorobo having his tiny house on top of a big tree in Kericho (Kenya) just like he loves a chief executive officer transacting business at the New York Stock Exchange. No one is less important in his sight. It is we human beings that have placed premiums on a superficial value system. I believe God enjoys a variety of worship—whether from hymnbooks or songs accompanied with clapping and dancing. We do not have any right to judge, because songs are not directed to us anyway.

Jesus made it clear that believers will be persecuted in the world but that they should cheer up because he has overcome the world. One way to walk through this world that's full of persecution is to always purpose to see the exalted view of God—His splendor, His majesty, His glory, and His power. When God is exalted in our lives, every persecution and problem we go through will not be too heavy to bear. Praise and worship is the means of exalting the Lord of Lords and the King of Kings.

Prayer and Works

For it is by grace you have been saved, through faith - and this not from yourselves, it is the gift of God—not by works, so that no one can boast. For we are God's workmanship, created in Christ Jesus to do good works, which God prepared in advance for us to do. ~ Ephesians 2:8-10

From this text, it is clear that good works cannot save us. It is also true from the text that after salvation, we are supposed to do good works. We can't just pray and expect everything to come to us on a silver plate. Many times we will have to work in order to get what we are praying for.

We must be willing to pray, work and to pay the price even if everything is against us. Remember:

- Milton wrote the greatest literature when he was blind.

- Helen Keller became deaf, dumb and blind shortly after birth, only to become one of the world's greatest motivational writers.
- Beethoven wrote some of the world's greatest music when he was deaf.
- Albert Einstein did not speak until he was four years old and couldn't read until he was seven. Zurich Polytechnic refused to admit him because he 'showed no promise'.
- Winston Churchill flunked sixth grade and several college courses.

The fact that things look hard is not reason enough to give up. We have to commit things to God in prayer and at the same time seek the door that the Lord is opening.

I have known believers who are good at praying but not willing to walk out of their prayer closet to see the door the Lord has already opened. While in college, we had a brother who was a real prayer warrior. The problem was that he was not willing to work hard in class. He would be busy praying while others attended a lecture or completed their laboratory practical. His habit of not attending class continued for some time so when exams came, he failed miserably. God is not glorified when his child has failed exams. Praying to God is not more spiritual than working hard to glorify God. We must both pray and work if we are to receive the promises that God has given us.

Importance of Work

Lazy hands make a man poor, but diligent hands bring wealth. He who gathers crops in summer is a wise son, but he who sleeps during harvest is a disgraceful son. ~Proverbs 10:4-5

We have to be hard working in order to make wealth. The Bible is categorical here that sleeping during harvest is a disgrace. Praying and working should be viewed as mutually inclusive and complimentary as opposed to being exclusive.

You can to do a comparison study between different countries in order to appreciate the importance of hard work. Start by contrasting Japan and Somali. Japan has a population of 126 million people and a land area of 374,744 kilometers. In other words, in every square kilometer, you find 335 people. On the other hand, Somali has a population of 9.9 million and a land area of 627,340 square kilometers, meaning in every square kilometer, you will find 16 people. From these statistics, you would expect that Somalia should be doing better economically since they have more land and by implication, resources compared to Japan. But this is not the case. The standard of living is much higher in Japan compared to Somali mainly because of the good work ethics of the Japanese. The Japanese work so hard and many of them get just four hours of sleep every day—this is not the case in Somali. I know you might be saying "But they have not had a government for the last fifteen years'—well, even when they had a government, Japan was ahead of them in many ways.

To reinforce my point, I will draw a dichotomy between one of the largest countries in Africa: the Democratic Republic of Congo (formerly Zaire) and the Netherlands. DRC (Democratic Republic of Congo) has a population of 47.7 million people and land area of 2,267,600 square kilometers. This means that the population density of DRC is 21 people per square kilometer. Netherlands on the other hand has a population of 15.6 million people and land area of 33,920 square kilometers. Population density of Netherlands is 461 people per square kilometer. Despite the high population density in the Netherlands that should lead to a depletion of resources, people in the Netherlands continue to enjoy a better life compared to their counterparts in DRC. It is interesting to know that DRC is endowed with lots of minerals and yet millions of its population still languishes in poverty. The problem basically lies in the lack of hard work and, to a greater extent, leadership problems.

Service

Paul makes it clear in Ephesians 4:11-12: *It was he who gave some to be apostles, some to be prophets, some to be evangelists, and some to be pastors and teachers, to prepare God's people for* ***works of service****, so that the body of Christ may be built up.*

From this portion of scripture, it is clear that we are to serve. Serving is all about working on the behalf of others. Prayer is not meant to be a substitute for work. We see works of service in Acts 6:3: *Brothers, choose seven men from among you who are known to be full of the Spirit and wisdom. We will turn this responsibility over to them....*

We need to understand that these were spiritual people who would have 'spiritualized' issues and said 'let us pray that the needs of the widows be met'. Other than giving themselves to the ministry of prayer and the word, they thought it wise to initiate something that would help the widows. I think we can learn a lot from the apostles' decisions. The church cannot afford to sit on the fence and watch people die of HIV/AIDS and hunger without extending a hand of love through good works. The recent drought that affected many parts of Kenya, especially the North Eastern province, was a good opportunity for the church to show love by providing relief food. This act went a long way in dispelling the rumor that Christians hate Muslims.

Our works will open doors that nothing else will. People are looking for individuals that are ready to help meet their needs. The church as an institution needs to graduate from just providing relief (feed me) to development (I can feed myself) and finally to business (creating wealth for others). Simply put: from receiving fish to fishing and finally to owning a fish farm.

Politics

There are things to pray about and also things to act upon as per the leading of God. I am impressed at what the church in Uganda is doing to fight pornography. In 2003, while visiting there, the church was unhappy with some magazines that were full of pornography. Other than praying about it, the church felt it should do something about it. Believers from different churches were mobilized to have a demonstration against a notorious magazine that was making quite a fortune by exposing nudity. People turned up in large numbers to express their displeasure at the magazine. In Kampala streets when all this was happening, it was exciting to see believers carrying placards denouncing the magazine. This well organized group of demonstrators later gathered together outside Uganda parliament to give the attorney general their demands that included the banning of the magazine. The point had been made—the church was not going to take the decay lying low.

I also give credit to those clergy in Kenya who organized a demonstration to protest against the legalization of abortion. The pro-choice groups had been aggressively advocating for legalization of abortion and everything seemed to be in their favor until the church stepped in and said it would not accept murder of children in the name of pro-choice. The church prayed against legalization of abortion and at the same time did something about it. Prayer and works are supposed to be intertwined. We have to listen to the leading of God before we take any course of action.

An organization called Kenya Church is a good case study for those who want to know more about prayer and works. They get credit for being exemplary in the area of mobilizing people to pray for Kenya and at the same time taking action against things that would affect the church and the people negatively. Kenya Church is a conglomeration of churches in Kenya who have come together to talk with one voice on issues of national importance. This group played and continues to play a critical role in the process of constitution writing in Kenya. Kenya Church is responsible for the inclusion of God's sovereignty in our land in the preamble of the proposed constitution. They also fought tirelessly against the inclusion of marriages of people of the same sex, Kadhis courts, and abortion, among other things.

Kenya church must have realized that when we pray we must be ready to act as per the leading of God without any fear. For once, Kenya has a group of people with microscopic eyes on the things happening in Kenya in order to commit them to God in prayer and act on God's leading. My prayer is that people reading this book everywhere in the world will be inspired to combine prayer and work.

It is a paradox that schools that have continuous strikes and fights have churches located not far from them. I sometimes think that those churches have taken prayer and other church activities as an excuse so they do not do what they are supposed to be doing. Such churches should be working in partnerships with those schools. They are the ones to take the good news to those schools so lives of the students can be transformed. I do not think honest headmasters and headmistresses would refuse having programs in their schools if they knew that it was going to benefit their students. The church is best able to address the problems of drugs and immorality among the youth. Apart from praying against such things in schools and institutions, we ought to take certain steps as per the leading of the Lord.

One area that has bothered me over the years on this issue of prayer and works is that of elections. Elections provide people with an opportunity to choose people they want to lead them over a given period of time. In Kenya and many other countries, it is five years. Believers have been praying that God would give them the right leaders for quite sometime in Kenya during election periods. Come election time, believers are nowhere close to the ballot box—perhaps praying still! We fail to learn from Ecclesiastes 3:1-8: *There is a time for everything, and a season for every activity under heaven: a time to be born and a time to die, a time to plant and a time to uproot, a time to kill and a time to heal, a time to tear down and a time to build, a time to weep and a time to laugh, a time to mourn and a time to dance, a time to scatter stones and a time to gather them, a time to embrace and a time to refrain, a time to search and a time to give up, a time to keep and a time to throw away, a time to tear and a time to mend, a time to be silent and a time to speak, a time to love and a time to hate, a time for war and a time for peace.*

I believe there is a time to pray and a time to act. We leave voting to be done by those who are not God fearing, and they end up electing their favorites. There is an English saying that states "birds of the same feathers flock together." Do not expect non-believers to choose saints as their leaders. In many cases they will choose those who bribe them. After bribing their way into parliament, these leaders resort to grand corruption and the believer has another prayer item to add to his long list—prayer against corruption in the government.

All these problems could have been averted if believers prayed for the election and then turned out to vote for people of integrity.

In many African countries, leadership problems are exacerbated by the fact that Christians view politics as a dirty game—something to be prayed for but not to be involved in. Because Christians shy from contesting political seats, non-believers end up getting into parliament and bring about legislations that end up hurting the church.

I like what happened in Kenya during the 2002 election. Believers realized that other than praying, they needed to vote. Pastors told their congregations why it was important to vote and to contest for political seats. The rumor that politics is a dirty game was dispelled. A number of believers sailed through the elections and have brought about positive change in the government. 'Prayer breakfasts,' organized by parliamentarians are now a familiar thing in Kenya. People have been enlightened on the need to have believers in parliament and it is just a matter of time before believers dominate the parliament in Kenya---I am looking forward to this.

Preaching

Preachers and teachers of the word should also pray and at the same time, work hard preparing what to feed God's people with. I get disappointed seeing preachers aggressively flipping through the scriptures a few minutes before the message time. It is okay if he is reminding himself of something but it is serious if he is coming up with a message at the time.

Do your best to present yourself to God as one approved, a workman who does not need to be ashamed and who correctly handles the word of truth. ~2 Timothy 2:15

Studying is hard work. If we are to bring a message that will bring revival in the hearts of the people then we must be ready to work at it. Lazy people are not willing to pay the price and would rather preach the same thing they preached somewhere else. We should be ready to wrestle with God until we find a word in season both for us and the people we are ministering to. If you are yearning to be used of God then you must be willing to throw laziness out the window and embrace hard work.

God himself is a hard worker—remember he worked for six days before resting on the seventh day. Some people do not deserve rest because they never work. Because God worked, you do not have any excuse why you should not.

Prosperity

In order for us to prosper, we must work. I know there has been a lot of talk about prosperity in our generation and I do not have any problem with that because I know God wants me to prosper. I admit that sometimes I think we are overemphasizing prosperity. My attitude has always been that of seeking his kingdom and righteousness first and all these other things. Some people take consolation in the preaching of prosperity and forget the flipside of the coin that we must also work for what we want.

Proverbs 12:24 says, *Diligent hands will rule, but laziness ends in slave labor.* Verse 27 of the same chapter says, *The lazy man does not roast his game, but the diligent man prizes his possessions.*

From these scriptures, we learn that laziness will lead to poverty, even if we have heard numerous sermons on prosperity and spend hours in prayer. It is little wonder then that believers are working for non-believers, many of who hardly have time to sleep because they are busy working round the clock.

The sluggard craves and gets nothing, but the desires of the diligent are fully satisfied. ~Proverbs 13:4

To me, this sounds like a spiritual law. We know about natural laws like the Archimedes principle—light bodies will float on water and heavy ones will sink. Spiritual laws are just as applicable as natural laws and are never violated. The law here is that if you are a sluggard you'll get nothing and if you are diligent, your desires will be satisfied.

Again I want to draw your attention to Exodus 17:8-13: *The Amalekites came and attacked the Israelites at Rephidim. Moses said to Joshua, "Choose some of our men and go out to fight the Amalekites. Tomorrow I will stand on top of the hill with the staff of God in my hands." So Joshua fought the Amalekites as Moses had ordered, and Moses, Aaron, and Hur went to the top of the hill. As long as Moses held up his hands, the*

Israelites were winning, but whenever he lowered his hands, the Amalekites were winning. When Moses' hands grew tired, they took a stone and put it under him and he sat on it. Aaron and Hur held his hands up - one on one side, one on the other - so that his hands remained steady till sunset. So Joshua overcame the Amalekite army with the sword.

It is important to note that prayer was vital for winning this battle. In fact, every time Moses lowered his hands, they were losing the battle. You must realize that he was not just praying alone. The Israelites had to fight with swords. In verse 13, it says that *Joshua overcame the Amalekite army with the sword.*

Ministry

God always grants victory through his people. Somebody once said that what we need to do is to be F.A.T. (Faithful, Available, and Teachable) so that God may use us. The above story is a perfect example of how prayer and works should go hand in hand if we are to have victory. Pastors need to try prayer and works together to experience something like a magic bullet. Many pastors have been praying for God to add to their numbers. They have fasted over this issue and it seems like nothing has happened. They are wondering because they are sure they have done everything right according to the practical workbooks they have. Well, my solution to them is that it is now time to get out of the closet and go to the 'world' where the sinners are and share with them about Jesus. It is time to work. We should see results if we are genuinely seeking God's face and aggressively preaching the gospel.

I must remind you that the intention of this topic is not to negate prayer but to strengthen it by way of introducing works as a complimentary tool. I must emphasize that a church that is working hard without seeking God's face by way of prayer will not be fruitful in the long run. What the church is doing is God's work and that must be done God's way and the only way to know his way is by seeking his face. The church that prays for the sick during their services is doing good but it is really great for them to visit those sick people in the hospitals; buy them gifts, and be of assistance to them at God's leading. This type of work often calls you out of your comfort zone to places you do not want to go. Missionaries who brought Christianity to Africa had great impact because of their works of goodness to the local people. They built schools, dispensaries, and churches for them. They also brought clothes and blankets to them. When the locals saw these people provide food for them, treat them free of charge and teach them for free, they realized that these people had a special kind of love for them and they in turn embraced the message they had. It is their works that revealed what was in them and people desired to have what was in their hearts. If you are wondering where we got lost on the way then I suggest that it is perhaps because we rubbished works and put emphasis on 'spiritual' things. We see works mentioned in Ephesians 2:8-9: *For it is <u>by grace</u> you have been saved, through faith -- and this not from yourselves, it is the gift of God --- <u>not by works</u>, so that no one can boast.* I think this scripture has been extrapolated so far that some have distorted it. These verses are clear that works cannot save us. Doing good cannot be good enough to enable us to merit God's kingdom. It is purely by God's grace through faith that we are saved. But then, good works also should not be rubbished. After receiving Christ, we must do good works that God prepared in advance for us to do. It is time that believers go back to the basics and let the presence of Jesus in us push us to do good works. The Bible makes it clear that wherever Jesus went, he did good. He fed people, healed the sick, raised the dead, and delivered demon possessed people. Jesus is the greatest prayer warrior of all times and in fact is interceding for us day and night (Hebrews 7:25). Besides prayer, his good works drew people closer to him than anything else. There are countries that will not accept approaches such as crusades, films, revival meetings, etc, because they are commonly called 'closed countries'. These 'closed countries' are, however, open to good works, and that is why I encourage churches and Christian organizations to consider doing relief work and development projects in these countries. People can resist many things, but they cannot resist the power of love. Our love packaged in good works will go a long way in opening doors that would otherwise remain closed. Think about the needs of the people and try to meet those needs.

It is shameful that those who do not know God have a passion to assist humanity more than those in the church. Surely, something is wrong and needs to be fixed. Living in denial cannot be a solution to any problem. The body of Christ must begin by accepting the problem and then asking God to forgive us and give us a fresh start. I know you might be saying, "But we do not have resources to do all that." Well, there are small things that you could do that will not cost you any money. All it requires is your time and energy. As a church in town, you could organize to clean your city—you just need rakes and gloves to do this exercise. You will need to get in touch with the town or urban council to assist you with logistics. If you are living in the village, you could organize to dig pit latrines for the people, teach them about good hygiene to protect them from diseases or even organize tree planting with the villagers. These events may not cost you any money but will go a long way in giving the church a good name in your town or village.

Good works should be at the institutional level and also at a personal level. There are things that we can do that will give us acceptance with our neighbors and that are a good opportunity for us to share about the love of Christ. Our prayer for their salvation will come to pass if we are busy doing things that are bringing them closer to God.

In conclusion, we must seek God's face by way of prayer in everything—the Bible actually tells us to pray without ceasing (1 Thessalonians 5:17). We also ought to do good works as per the leading of God. We must pursue both prayer and good works. I congratulate brothers and sisters who have prayed and excelled at working hard in the mission field, in academics, in business, in farming and in all other fields. May God help us to depend fully on him and at the same time come out of laziness and work hard for his glory.

Prayer and Faith

When praying, faith is the means by which we transact business in heaven just like money is the means of transacting business here on earth. Try getting goods out of a supermarket without money and you will realize how it is impossible to get anything from God without faith. Prayer without faith does not get any answer from God.

But when he asks, he must believe and not doubt, because he who doubts is like a wave of the sea, blown and tossed by the wind. That man should not think he will receive anything from the Lord; he is a double-minded man, unstable in all he does. ~James 1:6-8

This is a spiritual principle that always applies just like the natural law of gravity is applicable everyday. If you throw a stone up it shall surely come down.

Without faith you cannot please God and praying without faith is an exercise in futility. The biblical definition of faith is found in Hebrews 11:1: *Now faith is being sure of what we hope for and certain of what we do not see.* Nobody has ever seen the wind but its evidence is everywhere. Faith is the evidence of things hoped for. So you can have a better understanding of what I am talking about: You come to my house and I give you a seat. I think you will just sit on it because you have faith that it will support your weight. I would be amused beyond measure if you started doing scientific tests to verify whether the seat is strong enough to support you. By sitting on the seat, you are in essence saying that you trust the chair and that you are committed to that trust. Another example is that of an airplane trip. When you are boarding a plane, you can never be 100% sure that you will reach your destination. After the plane has been serviced and the engineers have checked it out, the probability that you will reach your destination is about 93%. Now faith is your commitment to the 93% probability. Faith in God comes from the knowledge of God as revealed in the scripture—in other words you have to believe that what is said in the Bible is true. I know that some people have given faith a wrong dimension and imply that you can have faith in faith. This is not biblical. Remember that we are not saved by faith but by grace through faith.

For it is by grace you have been saved, through faith-and this not from yourselves, it is the gift of God-not by works, so that no one can boast. ~Ephesians 2:8-9

Abraham

You cannot talk of faith without remembering the father of faith, Abraham. Abraham was told to leave his family and country to go to a land he knew not, and he accepted because he knew God was going to take care of his life. We see him and his wife Sarah living with the trauma of having no child. Later on when they are blessed with Isaac in their old age, God tells him to sacrifice his son. He is ready to do it because he has faith that God has the power to raise Isaac from the dead. Romans 4:20-21 concludes the life of the father of faith. *Yet he did not waver through unbelief regarding the promise of God, but was strengthened in his faith and gave glory to God, being fully persuaded that God had power to do what he had promised.*

One thing I like about God is that he has the power to do what he has promised. Fellow men might give you promises but the problem is that they sometimes lack the power to fulfill those promises. Some also will promise things that are blatant lies. I once heard a story of a high school student who promised his girlfriend a plane. This young man was actually extremely poor and did not even own a bicycle. But as for our God, the Bible says of Him in Psalm 24:1, *The earth is the Lord's, and everything in it, the world, and all who live in it.*

When praying, we must realize that God owns everything and that he loves us and is willing to grant us the desires of our hearts. If our prayer is full of doubts then it implies that we are not sure God has what we are asking for or that even if he has, we are not sure if he is willing to give it to us. Prayers of faith, on the other hand, agree that God owns everything, loves us and is willing to answer our requests. Prayers of faith appreciate Jeremiah 29:11, *'For I know the plans I have for you,' declares the Lord, 'plans to prosper you and not to harm you, plans to give you hope and a future'.*

Abraham knew that God had good plans for his life even when God told him to sacrifice his son Isaac. As human beings, we see a lot of promises ignored and unfulfilled by our friends or relatives. We also see weaknesses among ourselves in terms of our inability to do what we have promised, and it is very easy for these things to shape our thinking about God. We must realize that God has everything, is able, is faithful, is loving and will honor his promises.

In Numbers 13:1, an account of how Moses sent twelve men to spy out the land in order to bring back a report about the route they were to take and the towns they were to come to. Those twelve men went up into the hill country, and came to the valley of Eshcol and explored it. All twelve men were in consensus that the land the Lord was giving them was good—flowing with milk and honey. However, it emerged that there were two categories of people there, one made up of Joshua, son of Nun and Caleb, son of Jephunneh; the other group was made of the other ten gentlemen. Joshua and Caleb were people of faith and believed that God was able to fight for them and give them the land. The other fellows only saw the powerful people in those lands, the descendants of Anak and the fortified cities.

Opportunity

In the world, we have two types of people: those who are optimistic and those who are pessimistic. The former group sees opportunity in everything including a crisis while the latter group sees trouble even where there is none. If you take two people, an optimist and pessimist into a forest, the one who is optimistic will see opportunity to get timber out of the forest. He will also see wood that can be burnt for charcoal and sold dearly. (I am not encouraging forest destruction.) The pessimists, on the other hand, will keep talking about the snakes and the lions in the forest. A prayer of faith is the one that comes from a heart that is optimistic even if everything else is set against you. Because of the faith of Joshua and Caleb, they were able to enter into the Promised Land while the rest perished in the desert.

Prayer made out of faith will attract an answer. James 5:15 says, A*nd the prayer offered in faith will make the sick person well; the Lord will raise him up. If he has sinned, he will be forgiven.*

By now, you must realize that prayer is not a pious collection of words that are meant for a show. We must mean what we are praying and trust that God is going to make it come to pass. The truth is that, humanly speaking; some of the things you will pray for will look difficult and almost impossible. Just remember that it is not by your might nor by your power but by the spirit of the Lord.

As a first year student at the University of Nairobi I met a young man called Gathiwa. We were classmates and met quite often. I was already a believer but Gathiwa was not. This young man was known for all the wrong reasons and he seemed to like it that way. I developed a burden to pray for him and share with him about the love of Christ and how accepting Christ would change him. Strangely, the more I prayed for him, the worst he became. It was so easy to give up on him but I had faith that somehow God would do something about this young man who was considered more sinful by other sinners. Every time I shared with him the gospel, he would just mock me. Gathiwa derived pleasure from belittling me and the message I carried. This went on for almost three and a half years, and there was no sign things would get any better. I hoped against hope that God would intervene in this situation.

One Friday night at 11 pm, coming from fellowship, Steve (my roommate) and I met Gathiwa on the corridor floor drunk and saying things that only he understood. I remember telling him, "Gathiwa, if only you knew God, your life would not be like this." Steve and I went into our room and left the young man lying on the corridor. It is hard to understand how God operates. A few minutes later, Gathiwa walked into our room and started narrating his story to us. Gathiwa thought that God was the one who spoke to him at the time I said 'Gathiwa, if only you knew God, your life would not be like this.' It seems God magnified my voice in Gathiwa's ear. But I was amazed that this young man in his drunken state found his way into our room because there were over two hundred rooms in that block!

We shared with him about the gospel while he was still drunk. He accepted to receive Christ in that state. I thought in my mind 'maybe he is not serious' but I refused to believe my thinking. Gathiwa was a serious believer, period! I did not want to believe anything less. The following day, I saw him with a huge smile on his face. He started attending fellowship at our Christian union and even shared about his encounter with the Lord. Other sinners did not believe him and thought that he 'would come back to his senses' and join them. He refused to accept offers of alcohol that his former friends were generously giving. Even his dressing style changed. Instead of tattered jeans, the man wore suits and looked very professional all the time.

Gathiwa's conversion did not come easy—three and a half years of praying and sharing with him. If it were not for faith in God, then I would have easily given up on the young man. I met Gathiwa recently—several years after his conversion, and he is still doing well in the Lord.

Patience

One big problem with us these days is that we want things fixed quickly. Even products from supermarkets do not help us with this 'real fast' syndrome. Get coffee; add water and you have instant coffee. Fast foods like french fries are in high demand compared to those foods that take longer to be cooked. Because our world seems to be running fast, we also want our prayers to be answered immediately. God does not work like this—he operates in his own time. It is true that sometimes God answers our prayers immediately. For example, the criminal who hung next to Jesus requested Jesus to remember him. Luke 23:43 says, *Jesus answered him, "I tell you the truth, today you will be with me in paradise."*

Other prayers will receive a 'No' answer as shown by David's story in 2 Samuel 11. David had sinned with Bathsheba and after she conceived he led a conspiracy that saw Uriah (the husband of Bathsheba) killed. His prayer and God's response is recorded in 2 Samuel 12:15-18: *"After Nathan had gone home, the Lord struck the child that Uriah's wife had borne to David, and he became ill. David pleaded with God for the child. He fasted and went into his house and spent the nights lying on the ground. The elders of his household stood beside him to get him up from the ground, but he refused, and he would not eat any food with them. On the seventh day the child died."*

Take note that we cannot manipulate God to get the exact thing that we want to have as an answer. Not even after much prayer and fasting can we arm-twist him.

Other prayers are answered after a delay as shown in Luke 18:1-7. It is a story of a judge who did not fear God nor care about men. A widow kept coming to him asking for justice against her adversary. For some time he refused. But finally he gave her justice because the widow kept bothering him. Verses 7 and 8 say, *And will not God bring about justice for his chosen ones, who cry out to him day and night? Will he keep putting them off? I tell you, he will see that they get justice, and quickly. However, when the Son of Man comes, will he find faith on the earth?*

The timing of the answer is not within our realm—it belongs to God. Ours is to have faith that he will answer us instantly, after a while, or even an answer coming in the form of a 'No'. He knows what is best for us because he knows the end from the beginning. His answer is what we need.

God Knows Best

Actually, God might choose to give you a totally different thing from what you prayed for as shown in 2 Corinthians 12:7-9. *To keep me from becoming conceited because of these surpassingly great revelations, there was given me a thorn in my flesh, a messenger of Satan to torment me. Three times I pleaded with the Lord to take it away from me. But he said to me, "My grace is sufficient for you, for my power is made perfect in weakness.*

Paul wanted the thorn removed, but God gave him the grace to live with it. God's answer is the best because he has infinite knowledge about everything. We are shortsighted and cannot see far.

I love the fact that God is knowledgeable about everything. I was privileged in 1999 to have taken military chaplains through training on evangelism and discipleship. Some of these people had masters in divinity and other fields and I was still a young fellow who had just completed my undergraduate course two years earlier. One of the chaplains wanted to outdo me and show that he was great. Not all military chaplains have a relationship with God — to some of them it is just a job like any other. So the man wanted to show that he knew more than I. What he did not know was that he was dealing with a Christian apologist. He asked me arrogantly, "Suppose I am an atheist, can you prove to me that there is a God?" The hall was dead quiet and a pen dropping would be heard by everybody. How I answered the question was going to deny me or give me credibility to minister to those scholars. My response? I asked him if he knew Mr. Johnson Okello, and he responded that he did not know him. "It is over," I told him! You cannot claim there is no God if you do not have infinite knowledge. I told him that Mr. Johnson Okello is my dad and that if he did not know him, then chances were that there is a God somewhere, but that he did not know it because of his limited knowledge. I went ahead and informed him that you can only have the audacity to say, "There is no God," if you know the names of all Chinese, know all the streets in Mexico and have knowledge about everything. The laughter that followed my answer made that chaplain so ashamed. I gained credibility to minister to them.

Having faith in God who is all-knowing is a very logical thing to do. Lack of faith in the word of God is a dangerous thing and leads to death.

2 Kings 6:24 shows how Ben-Hadad, king of Aram had mobilized his entire army and laid siege to Samaria. There was so much famine in the city that even a donkey's head sold for eighty shekels of silver and a quarter of a cab of seedpods for five shekels. The famine was so bad that some women determined to eat their sons. The situation was terrible. Hear what the prophet had to say

in 2 Kings 7:1: *Elisha said "Hear the word of the Lord. This is what the Lord says: About this time tomorrow, a seah of flour will sell for a shekel and two seahs of barley for a shekel at the gate of Samaria." The officer on whose arm the king was leaning said to the man of God, "Look, even if the Lord should open the floodgates of the heavens, could this happen?" "You will see it with your own eyes," answered Elisha, "but you will not eat any of it!"*

The officer looked at the situation they were in and could not fathom how God's word through Elisha was going to happen. If you are to have faith, then you must move your eyes off the circumstances and focus on God's word. We must stop living by sight and choose to trust his word more than what we see, hear, touch, and smell. We should incorporate faith as our sixth sense. Elisha's word came to pass in 2 Kings 7:16*: "Then the people went out and plundered the camp of the Arameans. So a seah of flour sold for a shekel, and two seahs of barley sold for a shekel as the Lord had said."*

The prophecy of the officer who chose doubt instead of faith also came true in 2 Kings 7: 19-20: *The officer had said to the man of God, "Look, even if the Lord should open the floodgates of heavens, could this happen?" The man of God had replied, "You will see it with your own eyes but you will not eat any of it!" And that is exactly what happened to him, for the people trampled him in the gateway, and he died.*

Believing the Impossible

What the officer forgot is that what is impossible with man is possible with God. Faith should replace doubt if our prayers are to be answered.

A classic example of amazing faith in the New Testament is that of the centurion in Matthew 8:5-10. *When Jesus had entered Capernaum, a centurion came to him, asking for help. "Lord," he said, "my servant lies at home paralyzed and in terrible suffering." Jesus said to him, "I will go and heal him." The centurion replied, "Lord, I do not deserve to have you come under my roof. But just say the word, and my servant will be healed. For I myself am a man under authority, with soldiers under me. I tell this one, 'Go,' and he goes; and that one, 'Come' and he comes. I say to my servant, 'Do this,' and he does it. When Jesus heard this, he was astonished and said to those following him, "I tell you the truth, I have not found anyone in Israel with such great faith."*

This man believed that the word of Jesus alone was enough to heal his servant. Great is the faith of the one that trusts in God's word.

Many times in the New Testament, Jesus commended the people for their faith. In Matthew 15:21-28: *Leaving that place, Jesus withdrew to the region of Tyre and Sidon. A Canaanite woman from that vicinity came to him, crying out, "Lord, Son of David, have mercy on me! My daughter is suffering terribly from demon-possession." Jesus did not answer a word. So his disciples came to him and urged him, "Send her away, for she keeps crying out after us." He answered, "I was sent only to the lost sheep of Israel." The woman came and knelt before him. "Lord, help me!" she said. He replied, "It is not right to take the children's bread and toss it to their dogs." "Yes, Lord," she said, "but even the dogs eat the crumbs that fall from their masters' table." Then Jesus answered, "Woman, you have great faith! Your request is granted." And her daughter was healed from that very hour.*

This woman was not willing to take anything less for an answer other than the healing of her daughter. I also realize from the above scripture that whether or not your prayer is answered is very much dependent on your faith.

Matthew 9:27-29: A*s Jesus went on from there, two blind men followed him, calling out, "Have mercy on us, Son of David!" When he had gone indoors, the blind men came to him, and he asked them, "Do you believe that I am able to do this?" "Yes, Lord," they replied. Then he touched their eyes and said, "According to your faith will it be done to you."*

These blind men had their sight restored because they believed Jesus could heal them. Many more in the Bible had healings because of their faith. Remember that faith is the means of transacting business with God just like money is the means of transacting business here on earth.

People who have had faith to trust God for what humanly speaking is impossible have seen God do great things. I think about the late Bill Bright together with his wife Vonnette. They were founders of Campus Crusade for Christ. Their motto was, "Reach the campus today, reach the world tomorrow." In the midst of financial limitations and other challenges, this couple had faith that God was able to allow them to reach the world with the gospel. Campus Crusade for Christ is now one of the largest Christian organizations in the world. The Jesus Film (a Campus Crusade for Christ tool for mass evangelism) has been translated into hundreds of languages, and billions of people have watched it. Millions of people have received Christ through this tool. It is amazing the things that God can use you to accomplish if you have faith in him.

Tributes of Faith

Hebrews 11 pays tribute to men and women of faith. Remember, by faith the people of Israel passed through the Red Sea as on dry land, but when the Egyptians tried to do so, they drowned. By faith the walls of Jericho fell after the people marched around them for seven days. I like the conclusion of Hebrews 11. Look at verses 32-40: *And what more shall I say? I do not have time to tell about Gideon, Barak, Samson, Jephthah, David, Samuel and the prophets, who through faith conquered kingdoms, administered justice, and gained what was promised; who shut the mouths of lions, quenched the fury of the flames, and escaped the edge of the sword; whose weakness was turned to strength; and who became powerful in battle and routed foreign armies. Women received back their dead, raised to life again. Others were tortured and refused to be released, so that they might gain a better resurrection. Some faced jeers and flogging, while still others were chained and put in prison. They were stoned; they were sawed in two; they were put to death by the sword. They went about in sheepskins and goatskins, destitute, persecuted and mistreated—the world was not worthy of them. They wandered in deserts and mountains, and in caves and holes in the ground. These were all commended for their faith, yet none of them received what had been promised. God had planned something better for us so that only together with us would they be made perfect.*

I hope that reading about these men and women of faith makes your faith grow. The fact that my prayer for Gathiwa was answered has made me realize that there is nothing impossible with our God. I can now trust him whenever I face a difficult situation. David's faith also grew when he saw God give him victory over a lion and a bear. He was ready for Goliath because he could bank on the same God who gave him deliverance in the past.

In 1 Samuel 17:33-37, *Saul replied, "You are not able to go out against this Philistine and fight him; you are only a boy, and he has been a fighting man from his youth." But David said to Saul, "Your servant has been keeping his father's sheep. When a lion or a bear came and carried off a sheep from the flock, I went after it, struck it and rescued the sheep from its mouth. When it turned on me, I seized it by its hair, struck it and killed it. Your servant has killed both the lion and the bear; this uncircumcised Philistine will be like one of them, because he has defied the armies of the living God. The Lord who delivered me from the paw of the lion and the paw of the bear will deliver me from the hand of this Philistine." Saul said to David, "Go, and the Lord be with you."*

Every time an issue confronted David and the Lord delivered him, his faith grew to another level. When confronted by Goliath, he recounted God's hand of deliverance in his life and that gave him faith to face this man that the Israelites feared so much.

Faith Overcomes Fear

Whenever you are in doubt or fearful of a situation you are facing, take a moment and remember some things that God has done. Reflecting on those things will raise your faith to trust that same God for victory in your situation. If you trusted God for a bicycle, you can now trust him for a car. After God has provided a car, it may not be hard to trust him for a plane if you are convinced you need it.

Fear of the unknown may cause us to be bound in one place making us totally unwilling to try something for God.

The story of Bekele Shanko (Director of Affairs of southern and eastern Africa—Campus Crusade for Christ) is a great example of what God can do through those who are willing to stretch their muscle of faith and trust God for greater things. As the director of the 'great commission' movement back in his homeland of Ethiopia, Bekele had the burning desire to saturate the whole city of Addis Ababa with the gospel in forty days. This was a big step of faith, and many of his colleagues could not fathom how the young man was going to accomplish the mission. The mission was dubbed 'Operation Philip' (remember the story in the Bible about Philip and the Ethiopian eunuch?). Some of his colleagues thought this idea was crazy and unrealistic and pulled out. People want to be involved in things that they know will work. Nothing deterred Bekele from pursuing what God had put in his heart. Pastors from different churches were mobilized and the vision shared with them. Laymen were trained on how they were to go about evangelism and discipleship.

On the set day, multifaceted approaches were adopted in reaching the city with the gospel. Strategies sharing the gospel including the 'Jesus Film', one to one personal evangelism, executive dinners, radio and television advertising, were employed for the forty days.

What was thought to be impossible became possible because of certain men and women of Ethiopia who looked beyond financial difficulties and other numerous challenges and fixed their faith in a mighty God.

When Bekele became the leader in southern and eastern Africa, he decided that what had happened in Addis Ababa through 'Operation Philip' could be replicated in major cities of the twenty-two countries under his leadership. His faith had grown and as David could recount God's hand of victory, Bekele's point of reference was 'Operation Philip'. Together with other leaders in the region, they came up with vision 50:50:50. According to this vision, fifty million people in South and East Africa were to be reached with the gospel in fifty strategic cities in fifty days. This mission was dubbed OSA (Operation Sunrise Africa). OSA resulted in millions of people making decisions for Christ, thousands discipled and thousands of churches being planted.

I challenge you to start praying for something so big that when it is done people will know that God is the one that has done it.

Other ways that your faith will grow reading the scriptures and interacting with other men and women of faith. Reading how God used weak people like Gideon in the Bible will encourage you because you will see yourself as not being an exception. Listening to people who trusted God for great things and God granted their prayers will also go a long way in strengthening your muscle of faith.

In conclusion, James 1:6-7 says, *But when he asks, he must believe and not doubt, because he who doubts is like a wave of the sea, blown and tossed by the wind. That man should not think he will receive anything from the Lord; he is a double-minded man, unstable in all he does.*

Whatever you are praying for, you must believe that you have it and never waiver from that trust.

Prayer and The Word

If our prayers are going to be answered, they must be in line with the word of God and not contradict it. Prayer is difficult for me if I do not study the word of God. Every time I have stayed away from the word for some time, I find my prayer life extremely dry—in fact, all I do is keep repeating the same words that are registered in my mind and yawn and finally give up praying.

Studying the word of God and meditating on it helps you know how best to pray according to the will of God.

Jesus' disciples asked him to teach them how to pray and he responded in Matthew 6:9-13, *This is how you should pray: "Our Father in heaven, hallowed be your name, your kingdom come, your will be done on earth as it is in heaven. Give us today our daily bread. Forgive us our debts as we also have forgiven our debtors. And lead us not into temptation, but deliver us from the evil one."*

Inherent in this passage of scripture is that God wants us to honor him with our prayers. Our God is a jealous God and does not share his glory and honor with anybody else. Prayer is meant to honor God.

The second thing we note in this model of prayer is that the focus of prayer should be to bring God's kingdom on earth—this means men and women coming under the authority and Lordship of our God.

We are sojourners here on earth and are not supposed to live as if our lives are not transient. Knowing that we are ambassadors representing God on earth should motivate us to pray for non-believers to accept Christ as their Lord and Savior. The most important thing that can happen to a person is when he/she makes the decision to invite Christ into his/her life. This act causes angels in heaven to abandon everything they are doing to join in celebration. People need prayer for healing, prayers for restoration of relationships, prayer for deliverance from oppressions of the enemy, prayers for prosperity, prayers for journey mercies and so forth. But the thrust of our prayers should be towards global evangelization so that the kingdom of God may be established in the hearts of all people. After all, receiving Christ will prepare them to begin living victorious Christian lives free from oppression of the enemy.

I have traveled to some 'closed countries' and learned a vital lesson that these nations need a concerted prayer of believers from all over the world in order for the kingdom of God to be established in these countries. I have testimonies of how some people in those countries have received Christ through visions, dreams and other miraculous ways. These occurrences happen because people are praying somewhere.

It is a great tragedy that our prayers are usually a shopping list to God. We have become so selfish and egocentric that everything revolves around us. Seeing that the kingdom of God is established should be our number one priority and this should be reflected in our prayers.

God's Will

Jesus taught his disciples that they should pray for the will of the Father to be done. The will of the Father is that we would have holiness, righteousness and justice reigning in the land. It is our responsibility to lift our nations up in prayer so that they may be godly nations. The Bible makes it clear that sin is a reproach to a nation but righteousness exalts a nation. Wickedness is on the increase in our nations and God abhors it. As I am writing this book, South Africa has just legalized marriages of people of the same sex. England is about to see the first wedding of people of the same sex.

I think you are terribly mistaken if you think that we are better off than Sodom and Gomorrah. No wonder calamities are striking every corner of the earth. Kenya has recently experienced an earthquake measuring 6.8 on the Richter scale. Several cities in East and Central Africa were affected by this tremor whose epicenter was at Lake Tanganyika, located on the border of Tanzania and the Democratic Republic of Congo. The last time Kenya experienced an earthquake was in 1928, and it measured 6.9 on the Richter scale. One thing to note is that there was a believer who had warned of an earthquake that was coming that would affect several cities in Kenya because of wickedness in the country. Many of us read about his warning but never took him seriously. Every city he mentioned was affected by the tremor. He had mobilized people to pray that God would withhold his wrath. I believe the prayer we made caused a difference; the impact of the earthquake would have been even more devastating.

From Jesus' model of prayer, our prayer must have the element of asking for forgiveness. We should ask forgiveness not only for ourselves but also our relatives, our friends, our neighbors, our nations and so forth. We are to ask God to lead us not into temptation---this recognizes the fact that we are weak and that only God's hand can keep us from the devices of the enemy of our soul.

Any prayer that is motivated by selfish interest at the expense of the word of God will not get an answer. I have heard people say prayers that I was sure were not guided by the word of God. Worse still, because of ignorance, some people have given 'testimonies' about the 'miracles' God did in their lives and yet when you try looking at the so called 'miracles', you come to the conclusion that it is not consistent with the word of God. The story of 'miracle babies' is still vivid in my mind. According to information in different newspapers in Kenya, it is alleged that there is a preacher who has been praying for barren women to get pregnant. The 'miracles' have been happening and quite a number of women say that they have experienced this 'miracle'. One thing about this story is that some of the babies have been born three months after conception and everything was normal, including the body weight. Some of the women who gave birth also claim they did not have any sexual encounters. These stories might sound great but we must realize that they are inconsistent with the principles in the Bible. For example, in order for a child to be born, there must be a union between a man and a woman. Jesus is the only exception because he is the Son of God. Naturally, children take about nine months in the womb.

Scriptural Ignorance

Heresies are already with us and we must reject them and pursue God's word.

2 Peter 2:1-2: *But there were also false prophets among the people, just as there will be false teachers among you. They will secretly introduce destructive heresies, even denying the sovereign Lord who bought them—bringing swift destruction on themselves. Many will follow their shameful ways and will bring the way of truth into disrepute.*

It is time to be like the Bereans who studied the Bible diligently. Every time the preacher shared, they would dig into the Bible to verify if what was shared was true. We lack the qualities of the Bereans in our days and we desperately need to cultivate the culture of studying the word of God.

I joke when teaching God's word that there are preachers who aren't quite sure whether it was Jonah who swallowed the fish or if it was the fish that swallowed Jonah. Being the crafty people they are, they always conclude, 'whichever the case, one must have swallowed the other'.

I once had a conversation with a religious leader in my village who told me that the Bible says, "God helps those who help themselves." I asked him to tell me which book in the Bible talked about this but he was not able to. It seems like people would rather read newspapers and other books than the word of God. The Bible makes it clear that the heavens and the earth will pass away but the word of God will abide forever.

I have talked to people who try to discredit the Bible but as I engage them in what they think are contradictions in the Bible, they come to accept that their arguments are hollow and do not hold water.

Any book claiming to be the truth must be logically consistent, must be non-contradictory, and must be supported by both the archeological and historical evidences. The Bible passes all these tests and is the only book that has withstood the test of time. Think of the accuracies of the fulfillment of the prophecies in the Bible—so exact to an extent that it is an embarrassment to those discrediting the Bible.

It is a great thing to know that the word of God is experientially relevant to me—it has changed me totally. The good thing about experiential relevance is that another person who never experienced it cannot negate it. The entrance of the word of God will surely bring life. Psalm 119:9-11 says, *How can a young man keep his way pure? By living according to your word. I seek you with all my heart; do not let me stray from your commands. I have hidden your word in my heart that I might not sin against you.*

Hiding the word of God in our hearts protects us from sinning against God and when we go to him in prayer, he listens to us.

Praying the Scripture

One practice that I have found very helpful in enabling me to pray according to the will of God is that of taking certain portions of scripture and praying them back to God. For example, if the enemy has surrounded you and is threatening to finish you, then you can turn to Psalm 91 and say a prayer like this: "Thank you, Lord that I dwell in your shelter and in your shadow. You are my refuge and my fortress, my God, in whom I trust. Lord, save me from the fowler's snare and from the deadly pestilence. Cover me with your feathers and let me find refuge under your wing. Your faithfulness is my shield and rampart. I will not fear the terror of night nor the arrows that fly by day…." This mode of prayer does not have to be word by word but you can adjust and adopt it according to the situation at hand. I have found many chapters in Psalms and other books rich in words that we can pray back to God. This mode of prayer will make your prayer life more meaningful as you will avoid vain repetitions of words.

We have to store the word of God in us so that our prayers will be full of his word. God's word is the one thing that can bring the difference in our lives because it has the power to create. Psalm 33:9, *For he spoke, and it came to be; he commanded, and it stood firm.*

It is time to establish things through prayer that are guided by the word of God. Through the word of God, we can rule the affairs of our nations as indicated in Jeremiah 1:9-10. *Then the Lord reached out his hand and touched my mouth and said to me, "Now, I have put my words in your mouth. See, today I appoint you over nations and kingdoms to uproot and tear down, to destroy and overthrow, to build and to plant."*

It is time we stopped blaming politicians for the mess we find ourselves in because as God's children, we are the ones entrusted with the responsibility of destroying wickedness and planting righteousness — we are to model it, and if there is a mess then the buck stops on our doorstep. It is time the world started experiencing our presence. Our absence in determining the affairs of the world has been very conspicuous.

Sometimes you wonder if the statistics we have about the number of believers in our countries are true given the paradoxes associated with it. Think about Rwanda being a Christian country yet during the genocide, Hutus and Tutsis slaughtered one another. Kenya is known to be 80% Christian yet is being ranked among the most corrupt countries in the world. There seems to be a gap somewhere, and prayer guided by the word of God will help fix the problem.

Sometimes I am disappointed to see that people of other faiths are more committed to their books than Christians are to the Bible. Many of those religious people have memorized their whole book, and yet we find it hard to memorize a chapter in the Bible.

While praying through the word, you also have to create time to listen to God. Remember that prayer is communication with God—meaning God also wants to speak to us.

Promises

God's word is always true and will come to pass regardless of how long it takes. Actually, sometimes in your prayer, God will tell you something about your life and immediately you might begin experiencing the exact opposite of what you have been told. Do not worry, because God's word will surely come to pass regardless of the obstacles you might face on the way. A good example of a man who faced difficulties after God had promised him a wonderful destiny is Joseph. Genesis 37 gives us an account of how Joseph saw in a dream that his sheaf was going to rise and stand upright while those of his brothers were going to gather around his, bowing down to it. In another dream, he saw the sun and moon and eleven stars bowing down to him—in other words, Joseph saw that he was going to be a ruler. Joseph must have thought that it was all about climbing a ladder from that very moment. But he was mistaken. The young man found himself in a cistern—this in itself was God's protection upon this lad for according to the original conspiracy, he was to be killed. God would not allow him to die before his word came to pass.

Joseph must have been wondering in the cistern, 'Lord, I thought you promised I was to climb the ladder; how come I am in a pit?' There are a lot of paradoxes in the Bible. If you want to be exalted, you must humble yourself, and if you exalt yourself, you will be abased. If you are ready to lose your life, you will gain it, and if you try to protect it, you will lose it. In Joseph's case, the paradox is what I call 'the way up is down'. You will climb the ladder if you are ready to go down. We see the same thing happening to Joseph at Potiphar's house---just when things are working fine for him, he finds himself in prison. But as I said earlier, God will watch over his word to perform it. In Genesis 41:41, Pharaoh elevates Joseph to be in charge of the whole land of Egypt. God's word (through the dream) came to pass in due time.

Joseph chose to hide God's word in his heart so as not to sin against God. In Genesis 39:9, *No one is greater in this house than I am. My master has withheld nothing from me except you, because you are his wife. How then could I do such a wicked thing and sin against God?* God honored the faith of this young man.

Isaiah 55:11 says, *So is my word that goes out from my mouth. It will not return to me empty, but will accomplish what I desire and achieve the purpose for which I sent it.*

Meditation on the Word

In order for us to hide the word of God in us, we need to meditate on his word. Through meditation, we reflect on God's word so it becomes part of us. Meditation entails listening to God. We live in a world that is so noisy that it can be hard hearing properly what the Master is telling us. Everybody wants their voice to be heard but do not want to listen to others. We forget the reason why God gave us two ears and one mouth — we are supposed to talk less and listen more, but what we see around us shows that the opposite is true. In many prayer meetings, you will find people taking a lot of time talking to God and immediately when they are done, they walk out without giving God time to speak to them too.

The difference between Christianity and other world religions is that Christianity is about a relationship in which God is reaching down to us while religion is man trying to reach God through religious rituals, good works and other efforts. God wants to speak to us through his word, so we need to meditate on it.

Talking and listening must go together. One reason why we have a lot of marital problems and even divorce in the world is because of communication breakdowns. Not many of us are good listeners. As the other person is explaining his/her part of the story, we are busy planning an appropriate answer even before understanding things fully. The world value system has also worsened the situation by putting premiums on eloquent talkers.

Some of the highest paid people in our nations are those that host talk shows, debates, etc. where the whole business is all about talking.

God reveals his purpose for his children as they are praying. *When I returned to Jerusalem and was praying at the temple, I fell into a trance and saw the Lord speaking. "Quick!" he said to me. "Leave Jerusalem immediately, because they will not accept your testimony about me." "Lord," I replied, "these men know that I went from one synagogue to another to imprison and beat those who believe in you. And when the blood of your martyr Stephen was shed, I stood there giving my approval and guarding the clothes of those who were killing him." Then the Lord said to me, "Go, I will send you far away to the Gentiles."* ~Acts 22:17-21

God revealed his purpose for Paul while he was praying, and this revelation shaped Paul's entire ministry.

I am sure you can appreciate the importance of God's word in prayer, but just in case you find it hard to pray to God using the Bible, get a friend and decide on a chapter in the Bible you will use in praying to God. Later I have included a chapter on how to build prayer movements wherever you go. But at this point, it is important to mention the method my wife Eunice has been using in regard to the word of God and prayer. Eunice is coordinating prayer in the region where we are and she has helped form a number of prayer cells that are praying for our town, country and the world. Every week, she gives all the cell leaders a scripture that guides them while praying throughout the week. People have found it great to base their prayer on the word of

God. Hebrews 4:12 makes it clear: *"The word of God is living and active. Sharper than any double-edged sword, it penetrates even to dividing soul and spirit, joints and marrow; it judges the thoughts and attitudes of the heart.* Wow, the word of God is so powerful, and we had better start using it in our prayers.

Defeating the Enemy

Jesus, when confronted by the enemy, resorted to the written word of God. In Luke 4:3-12, *The devil said to him, "If you are the Son of God, tell this stone to become bread." Jesus answered, "It is written: 'Man does not live on bread alone'." The devil led him up to a high place and showed him in an instant all the kingdoms of the world. And he said to him, "I will give you all their authority and splendor, for it has been given to me, and I give it to anyone I want to. So if you worship me, it will all be yours." Jesus answered: "It is written: 'Worship the Lord your God and serve him only'." The devil led him to Jerusalem and had him stand on the highest point of the temple. "If you are the Son of God", he said, "throw yourself down from here. For it is written: 'He will command his angels concerning you to guard you carefully: they will lift you up in their hands, so that you will not strike your foot against a stone'." Jesus answered, "It says: 'Do not put the Lord your God to the test'."*

From this scripture, Jesus defeated the devil by pointing out God's word. Every time the devil brought a temptation, Jesus spoke the word of God as the solution to that temptation, and the devil could not object. The word of God will always defeat the devil every time you use it. The word of God is our sword. Swords are meant for making offensive moves and not defensive. For a long time, we have been waiting for the enemy to attack us so we can defend ourselves, but the time has come and it is now here when we have to invade the camp of the enemy and attack with our swords.

The Bible promises that the gates of hell cannot prevail against the church — meaning that it is the church that is attacking. It is time to stop fearing the enemy, because we have the weapon that he cannot withstand — the word of God. The only reason the enemy can overcome you is if you choose to believe a lie instead of the word of God. He will keep telling you, 'you cannot make it,' 'it is not possible!" But deliberately choose not to believe his distortion of God's word, for if you believe his lie you will lose. *Now the serpent was more crafty than any of the wild animals the Lord God had made. He said to the woman, "Did God really say, 'You must not eat from any tree in the garden'?" The woman said to the serpent, "We may eat fruit from the trees in the garden, but God did say, "You must not eat fruit from the tree that is in the middle of the garden, and you must not touch it, or you will die." "You will not surely die," the serpent said to the woman.* ~Genesis 3:1-4

The great blunder of the woman was to allow the devil to argue with her over the word of God. We have to tell the devil what the word of God says with finality—no room for discussion. Discussing the word of God with the devil will give him opportunity to create doubt in you about the word and thereby make the sword blunt.

If you are sick in your body, turn to the word of God in Isaiah 53:4-5: *Surely he took up our infirmities and carried our sorrows, yet we considered him stricken by God, smitten by him, and afflicted. But he was pierced for our transgressions, he was crushed for our iniquities; the punishment that brought us peace was upon him, and by his wounds we are healed.*

In your prayers, declare yourself or whomever you are praying for healed based on God's word in the scripture. If you committed a sin and genuinely repented and asked God for forgiveness but the enemy is still haunting you with guilt then turn to the 'sword' and declare the words in 1 John 1:9: *If we confess our sins, he is faithful and just and will forgive us our sins and purify us from all unrighteousness.*

The enemy will lie to you that your sin was too big to be forgiven. Ignore his lie and embrace God's forgiveness. Make sure you are honest, that you in your repentance do not go back to the same sin because you will be taking God's grace for granted. This behavior is like putting Christ on the cross all over again—I am sure you do not want to do this.

Every situation you face in life has relevant scripture in the Bible that is meant to address it. It would be a great idea if you devised a schedule on how you will be studying and memorizing the word of God. I like the habit of memorizing scripture because it helps you store the word in your heart. You see, in order for your heart to accept something, your mind must have accepted it first. I am looking forward to the days when believers will be 'walking Bibles'. Other than memorizing the word of God, you must allow it to change you totally. We must not be as hard as a rock to an extent that God's word does not bring transformation in our lives. I remember some years back when I was in ministry at Makerere University in Uganda and sharing my faith with many students. The responses were overwhelming in terms of those who were receiving Christ, but there is one experience that is hard for me to forget. I was in a student's room and shared with him the gospel using the four spiritual laws booklet. After I was through, I asked him if he was interested in inviting Christ into his heart, and he responded by asking me to look for 'other fertile soils' because he was 'a hard rock'. Instead of feeling offended, I found myself amused by this response. The young man knew the story of Jesus' parable in Luke, chapter 8 and identified himself with the seed that fell on rocky soil. How I pray that you will be like a seed that falls on good soil yielding a crop, a hundred times more than was sown.

In conclusion, your prayer must be guided by the word of God if you are to get answers from the master. Saturating yourself with the word of God will enable you to offer the right prayers. For out of the abundance of the heart, the mouth speaks. Remember to use the word of God whenever the enemy strikes or wants to distort the word of God.

Prayer and Unity

The importance of unity cannot be overemphasized. It is amazing the kind of things we can do if we are united. Matthew 12 gives us an account where Jesus healed a demon-possessed man who was blind and mute so that he could both talk and see. Instead of the Pharisees praising God for his mighty works, they begin to accuse him that he was using the power of Beelzebub, the prince of demons. Look at Jesus' response in Matthew 12:25, *Jesus knew their thoughts and said to them, "Every kingdom divided against itself will be ruined, and every city or household divided against itself will not stand."*

Jesus made it plain that you cannot survive without unity—the enemy will easily defeat you.

I like watching animal documentaries. One thing I have learned is that even the king of the jungle (lion) finds it difficult to attack animals like hyenas if they are together. The lion will keep its distance hoping that one of the hyenas will stray away from the rest so the lion can prey upon it. If the animals are determined to stay together, then the lion will try tricks to divide them. A former president of the United States of America is remembered for his famous statement "United we stand, divided we fall". Our unity is our strength.

Not long ago I heard over the radio that some hyenas had joined together and killed a lion — that is the power of unity. What one hyena could not do, many of them working together did. United prayer yields great results.

Let us look at another classic example of what unity can do according to Genesis 11:1-6. *Now the whole world had one language and a common speech. As men moved eastward, they found a plain in Shinar and settled there. They said to each other, "Come, let's make bricks and bake them thoroughly." They used brick instead of stone, and tar instead of mortar. Then they said, "Come, let us build ourselves a city, with a tower that reaches to the heavens, so that we may make a name for ourselves and not be scattered over the face of the whole earth." But the Lord came down to see the city and the tower that the men were building. The Lord said, "If as one people speaking the same language they have begun to do this, then nothing they plan to do will be impossible for them."*

When you set out to do something in unity, you will accomplish it. Unity in prayer is what we need if we are to see God's kingdom established. It is good to pray as individuals, but it is better if we come together to pray.

United Prayer

There is something unique that happens when we pray together. The Bible makes it clear in Leviticus 26:8: *Five of you will chase a hundred, and a hundred of you will chase ten thousand, and your enemies will fall by the sword before you.* We find the Israelites being asked an important question in Deuteronomy 32:30, *How could one man chase a thousand, or two put ten thousand to flight, unless their Rock had sold them, unless the Lord had given them up?*

Ordinarily, if one chases a thousand you would expect two to chase two thousand but then this is not the case here as we see unity bring the multiplier effect. The synergy of a united prayer is what is going to destroy the idols that have masqueraded as gods of this world.

It is time we learn a simple lesson from termites. These tiny animals know that their survival is dependent on their unity. Their organizational skills and job divisions among themselves reflect greatly the genius of our God. Every member of this family plays its part so well that you are left marveling at the power of unity. The queen, male and female know exactly what their role is.

In football and other sports, people have to be united and work as a team in order for them to win the game. If you are playing football, you cannot be the goalkeeper and at the same time be the defender, midfielder and striker. Every person has a specific role they are playing, but they have to work as a team. The body of

Christ has worked as isolated parts for a long time—time has come for us to come together and pray together. Every believer must see other believers as brothers and sisters. It is time to know that all of us are laboring for the same Kingdom and the same Master. We cannot afford to engage ourselves in competition if our efforts are to be complementary.

As the body of Christ, we have to know exactly where we are going. In many churches, it seems like only the pastor knows the vision and the mission of the church while members are just passengers who aren't quite sure about their destination.

There was a time I mobilized believers that I was taking through training on evangelism and discipleship for a one week mission to a place that was about 150 kilometers from our town. After being in that area for a number of days, we visited a church to attend their Sunday service. Unfortunately for my trainees and my self, the church we attended was not organized. The pastor never appeared and it seemed people were just going to stay there for four hours waiting for someone whose whereabouts nobody knew. I decided I was not going to watch things of God going bad in my presence so I did everything----ushered people, led praise and worship, preached and then collected offerings. The good thing was that members of the church who attended that service received Christ after I invited them to do so if they did not have a relationship with the Master. It became clear that none of those people knew the Lord, and that God wanted the pastor to get distracted with other things so I would be able to present the truth to this group. All the same, I found it strange that a pastor could miss a service without giving any information to the members---there was no unity there. I finally gave the offering I had collected to the members to give to their pastor once he appeared from wherever he had gone. As children of the kingdom of God, we cannot afford to pull in different directions.

How good and pleasant it is when brothers live together in unity! It is like precious oil poured on the head, running down on the beard, running down on Aaron's beard, down upon the collar of his robes. It is as if the dew of Hermon were falling on Mount Zion. For there the Lord bestows his blessing, even life forevermore. ~Psalm 133

Unity Brings Blessing

Unity attracts the blessings of God. If we want to see God move and do great things in our lives then we have to strive to be united. Congratulations to those pastors who have formed pastors' fellowships in their cities in order to pray together and to compare notes on what they are doing so they do not duplicate what others are doing. Thank you also for those churches that have involved other churches in undertaking major projects they were doing. Let us encourage unity in everything we do.

The Colonialists were surviving with the tactic of divide and rule. They would collude with some locals, bring divisions amongst people that had hitherto lived in harmony and continue ruling. This is the same device that the enemy is using. The devil will keep bringing things that divide brother against brother so that they are not seeing each other eye to eye.

If we are to have unity once again then we have to allow the Lord to do radical surgery in us. We must ask God to remove the hatred we have harbored against one another. We have to confess the sins of bitterness, jealousy, pride, strife and every thing that might cause a problem between us and the other person.

I believe that God would want to see his church body united just as the Father, the Son and the Holy Spirit. It is our unity that will show the world that we belong to Him.

Make every effort to keep the unity of the Spirit through the bond of peace. There is one body and one Spirit—just as you were called to one hope when you were called—one Lord, one faith, one baptism; one God and Father of all, who is over all and through all and in all. ~Ephesians 4:3-6

Not Uniformity

We can be united in our diversity. Unity does not mean that all of us have to be the same, talk the same, sing the same, preach the same, dress the same and so forth. Unity comes about when we recognize the fact that we have the same hope, the same faith, the same Father, the same King, and the same Spirit.

One reason why we are having so much disunity is because many people have become carnal Christians. They no longer walk in the Spirit but they follow their own desires. Paul offers a strong rebuke for such people in Galatians 3:1-5: *You foolish Galatians! Who has bewitched you? Before your very eyes Jesus Christ was clearly portrayed as crucified. I would like to learn just one thing from you: Did you receive the Spirit by observing the law, or by believing what you heard? Are you so foolish? After beginning with the Spirit, are you now trying to attain your goal by human effort? Have you suffered so much for nothing—if it really was for nothing? Does God give you his Spirit and work miracles among you because you observe the law, or because you believe what you heard?*

Walking in the flesh has caused others to rebel against their pastors and start their own churches or ministries. I am not against the idea of starting churches. What I am against is allowing the enemy to plant seeds of division with your leader so you go your own way. It is possible for you to start a church or a ministry with the blessings of your leader—that way you will still be operating in the spirit of unity and doing some things together. The same problems that are causing divisions in our times are the same ones that caused divisions in Paul's days, and he addressed them in 1 Corinthians 3:1-4: *Brothers, I could not address you as spiritual but as worldly—mere infants in Christ. I gave you milk, not solid food for you were not yet ready for it. Indeed, you are still not ready. You are still worldly. For since there is jealousy and quarrelling among you, are you not worldly? Are you not acting like mere men? For when one says, 'I follow Paul,' and another, 'I follow Apollos,' are you not mere men?*

Paul gives a great analogy between the body and the church in 1 Corinthians 12:12-15: *The body is a unit, though it is made up of many parts; and though all its parts are many, they form one body. So it is with Christ. For we were all baptized by one Spirit into one body—whether*

Jews or Greeks, slave or free—and we were all given the one Spirit to drink. Now the body is not made up of one part but of many. If the foot should say, 'Because I am not a hand, I do not belong to the body,' it would not for that reason cease to be part of the body.

One common sin that has caused division is pride, the feeling that you are better than others, and that things can only be done well if you are the one who does them. This is a serious sin as it is the one that made the devil to be chased out of heaven by God. We need to keep evaluating ourselves if there is any trace of pride in us so we can ask God to forgive us.

Paul provides the antidote to division in 1 Corinthians 12:24b-27: *But God has combined the members of the body and has given greater honor to the parts that lacked it, so that there should be no division in the body, but that its parts should have equal concern for each other. If one part suffers, every part suffers with it; if one part is honored, every part rejoices with it. Now you are the body of Christ, and each one of you is a part of it.*

Our prayer must reflect the fact that we care for one another. We need to know what the whole body is going through and commit those issues to the Lord.

It is time to be concerned about the entire body. This will call upon you to do some research to know what the body of Christ is going through in Indonesia, Iraq, Pakistan, Afghanistan, Eritrea and so forth. It is wrong to be in our comfort zones without being concerned about our brothers and sisters who do not find it easy in certain countries—we must pray for them.

It is known that certain birds like to fly together. Some of those birds have been known to operate as a team. Those that are strong lead in front and they perch as the ones at the back honk to encourage them perching. Their perching removes any resistance of the wind so the ones at the back do not need to perch. When the ones at the front are tired, they take the back position, and the ones that were at the back have to take the responsibility of perching as the others take the role of honking to encourage—this is unity of purpose. Through this strategy, these birds are able to move long distances without feeling tired. Have you realized that when you are walking a long distance and there are two of you then you do not feel as tired as you would if you were alone? There is power in unity and we must strive for unity, in prayer so we can establish God's kingdom in the hearts of men.

Building Prayer Movements

A movement is an expanding group of people with a common objective. Some secular movements we know about include Maji Maji rebellion of Tanzania and Mau Mau of Kenya. In the case of Mau Mau, the objective was to drive away the colonialists. Mau Mau started as a small organization but gained momentum to become a powerful force to reckon with. These people, besides having inferior weapons compared to the ones of the British, the colonizers, were able to push things so hard that it later led to the independence of Kenya in 1963. True, some of them died, but that never cowed them from pursuing their goal. If anything, they had counted the cost and knew that lost lives were a part of the cost.

When it comes to prayer movements, the objective is to connect people to Christ's victory through prayer. We realize that spiritual conflict is real and that the only way to win is by inviting Jesus to fight for us. The enemy is destroying masses through cults, drugs, terrorism, HIV/AIDS, etc. and it is our responsibility as believers to have prayer movements that will call on God to deliver his people.

As mentioned earlier, my wife Eunice has been involved in building prayer movements where we are, and she has adopted a multifaceted approach in accomplishing this task. I hope that the sharing of how we help build prayer movements will make you initiate one in your area.

One good thing about building a prayer movement is that all the churches in our town are represented in the prayer movement. You might face challenges of involving other churches especially because there is suspicion existing among churches—we always see others as wanting to fish from our ponds. If you cannot involve members of other churches, you can go ahead and start with people from the church you attend, but it is ideal to have people from different churches.

We have good relationships with the pastors here and none of them doubt our motive. Our organization has created trust with them over the years. We realized that it was going to be very difficult to win people to Christ without first winning the battle in the spiritual realm. We recruited people into the group during prayer seminars, prayer rallies, and prayer retreats.

Prayer Seminars

In prayer seminars, people are taken through topics that make them see the need of prayer. After the seminar, we enlist names of those who are interested to join our prayer movement. The prayer group meets on a specific day every week for one hour to give thanks for prayers that have been answered and also to commit to the Lord new prayer items.

Our meeting time is between 1300 hrs to 1400 hrs every Monday. This is the time people are out for lunch, and so people forfeit their lunch to seek the face of the Lord.

When having prayer meetings, it is of great importance to observe time. In Africa, we are good at wasting time in the name of being led by the Spirit. The Spirit of God is orderly. If you keep going past time, you will lose many people because they do not want to be in a situation where their job is at risk because of arriving to work late. The best way to save on time is to have the person who is leading the meeting prepare in advance. Preparation entails typing the thanksgiving and prayer items before the meeting. The members of the movement will mention other items for prayer when prayer begins.

Try to involve all the members of the prayer movement in the different activities. You should consider having different people lead the meeting every time you meet; this is a way of developing prayer movement leaders.

In our case, because where we work is a very sensitive place, people are advised to keep typed prayer items safely out of sight or tear them up all together after use. The other preparation the leader needs to do is that of praying for those that will attend the meeting. Our Monday prayer meeting is run professionally and at the same time it is spiritual. It is hard having a meeting that lasts for an hour in a place where people are used to attending a service for five hours.

Prayer Tracking

One thing that we put priority on is that of tracking prayers. Tracking prayers is all about getting feedback to the prayer request God has answered. When we share what God has done, people's faith is strengthened, and they are encouraged to pray more. Some people think that prayer does not accomplish much, and so when they hear of the results of prayer they will choose to be aggressive intercessors instead of giving up praying. Tracking prayer also helps people to see what God has done so they can praise him and give him the glory.

Recently, we visited a couple that had just been blessed with a baby boy. Gideon had shared with us some years back their desire for a baby. We kept praying that God would grant the desires of their hearts. They finally had baby Victor. They were surprised that I remembered when Gideon shared with us the prayer item. It had been a long time, but I track prayers. The couple waited seven years and seven months before Victor arrived. Those who have not gone through this experience may not understand how painful and difficult it is to wait that long, especially if you are prepared to have a baby.

Openness is one thing that members of the prayer movement need to have. As the leader of the movement, you need to cultivate an environment where people know that whatever is shared will be private. Discourage members from engaging as 'spiritual gossips' in the name of sharing prayer items. The sharing should be for prayer and nothing else.

In order to have a proper prayer tracking system, you need to have a prayer file where prayer items and thanksgiving are recorded. Members of the group should access the prayer file any time they want. Remember that people's faith is strengthened when they see the answers to their prayers. You might wonder why many preachers talk about how God has used them to perform miracles—they are basically helping to raise the faith of the audience and at the same time encouraging them that if God did it in the past, he can do it now. So do not criticize preachers about the testimonies they are sharing.

Prayer Rallies

Another method of recruiting people into the prayer movement is through prayer rallies. In our case, we have been sending invitations to all the churches to attend the prayer rallies. Because we are dealing with different denominations, we always choose a venue that is neutral and acceptable to all. The intention of the prayer rally is not to recruit people into the movement but to actually pray. Recruitment of people into the prayer movement should be a by-product and not the focus of the prayer rally.

During the prayer rally, leaders from different churches bring their own prayer items. The prayer items should be prepared before the actual day of prayer to save on time. Some issues that we always pray for include: salvation of the local, unity of the church, peace in the nation, etc. Our prayer rallies usually run from morning to afternoon especially on a Saturday or any day that people are not attending work.

One way of praying during the prayer rally is prayer walking.

People pair up and take a walk in places that are being targeted. As you are walking, you observe the different needs you see and commit them conversationally to the Lord. One person should pray, and the other is to be in agreement. The prayer is done in such a way that other people seeing you will think that you are talking.

We serve as missionaries where Christians are in the minority (maybe 5%), and this has taught us to be extremely sensitive. Somebody once said that because men have learned how to shoot without missing, birds have learned how to fly without perching. We have learned to offer prayers without being noticed. Prayer walking is a great method of prayer because you get to see with your eyes the needs of people around you.

If prayer walking is not possible in your area, you might want to consider a 'prayer drive'.

In a prayer drive, you pray while driving. Together with two of my friends, we were able to cover in prayer all of the cities in a country that is 'closed'. We also drove through all the major towns in another 'closed country' next to the first one. These two experiences have made me appreciate prayer drives. As we moved around these countries, we kept praying that those people would be delivered from worshipping idols to worshipping the only true God---Jesus Christ. We also prayed for laborers to be sent to those countries (very few missionaries if any are in these countries) and for Christian radio stations to get opportunities to transmit the gospel of truth to these people who are in the dark.

Because of the security situation in one of those countries, during the prayer drive, we had a driver and a police officer who were not Christians. It is illegal for foreigners to travel without police escort there and therefore we had to devise a way of prayer that none of these people would hear. We just kept praying in our hearts for the needs that we saw as we drove.

It is also good to target your prayers. As earlier said, Jesus was a strategist who knew what to do in order to have the greatest impact. He ministered to the Samaritan woman and through her the whole city of Samaria learned about the message of the cross with quite a number believing the message of Jesus. We too can identify the strongholds of the wicked one in our cities and target them with prayers. Who knows? Maybe after surrounding them with our prayers they might come tumbling down like the wall of Jericho. For people who like jogging in the morning, how about turning it into 'a prayer jog'?

After the prayer rallies, it is good to give follow-up questionnaires to be filled out by the participants indicating things that they thought that needed improvement. Those who are interested in joining the prayer movements are recruited and requested to join the rest for the weekly prayer meetings. As indicated earlier, we are happy that all the churches have identified with our prayer movement. I really thank God for the unity of the church here. I always wonder why we do not have this sense of togetherness of the churches reflected in other places but I have realized that because we are the minority, our strength is in our unity. I also tend to think that persecution brings people together. Do not pray for it. In Acts of the Apostles, the church was just warm and not accomplishing much, but when persecution broke out, believers were scattered all over and they took the gospel wherever they found themselves.

You should share your burden of starting a prayer movement in your town with pastors so that they can give you their blessings. Make sure your motive is right as you go about prayer movement formation.

Prayer Retreats

'Prayer retreats' are another method of recruiting more intercessors into the movement. In prayer retreats, people gather for a time of prayer and later on they engage in games like volleyball, football, badminton, etc. At the end of the retreat, people are recruited to be part of the prayer movement. Make sure you get someone who is creative in making the games full of fun. These games make people bond together and bring a sense of closeness to one another. I have been amazed that pastors and elders really enjoy those games that remind them of their youth. Many people behave like they are too spiritual to play games. It is time to begin enjoying Christianity fully by having a good time together as a family.

Other Prayer Activities

Those who have been recruited into the movement are expected to attend the weekly meetings for one hour. They also join others in praying during the night. We have people in the group that have offered to wake up the rest during the night for prayers. We thank God for technology that has brought mobile phones. People are telephoned when their time for prayer is due. They are not supposed to answer the phone because answering it will mean the person who has called will lose money. The person calling just beeps briefly and stops when they are sure the person being called has heard. (Beeping takes 5 seconds).

Members of the prayer movement are also requested to observe the forty-day prayer focus every year. During this period of time, people pray for the salvation of locals. Some in the prayer movements choose to drink fruit juice for the entire period while others go on a supper only fast. Those who are too weak to manage the fast can skip breakfast only or even take the meals but keep praying for God's intervention in the entire world.

For quite sometime now, we have been forming twenty-four hour prayer chains for the entire period of the forty-day prayer focus. Every member of the movement is to choose one hour per day for the whole period of time when he can pray. After we have had all the twenty-four hours covered every day, we come up with a program of who will be waking up who (through beeping the phone). At night after you have prayed, you wake up the next person by calling him/her before you sleep. There is usually a list of everyone participating in the prayer focus and what time they are supposed to be praying. Telephone numbers of all the members are also included in the list so that when you are through with praying you call the next group of people who take over. The forty-day prayer focus has helped improve the prayer life of many believers. Many of them never thought they could manage to pray and fast for even a day. Now they have come to realize that they can do much more. It is very encouraging to know that other people are fighting the same battle as you, and so many people have been encouraged to fast.

During the forty-day prayer focus, we increase our meetings from once to twice a week. The extra hour at a prayer meeting is there to allow for a concerted prayer in order to pull down works of the evil one. There are always a lot of things happening in our town as the forty-day prayer focus coincides with Ramadan.

Other than people in our town, we always update our other friends about what to pray for and what to thank God for. Email is a great means of communication because at the touch of the button, you can communicate to many people and involve them in praying for different needs.

Prayer Cells

People in the prayer movements can form prayer cells. In our case, we have ten prayer cells at different geographical locations. Each prayer cell has a cell leader. Every cell group has the job description of calling on God on behalf of the people.

And when he had taken it [the book], the four living creatures and the twenty-four elders fell down before the Lamb. Each one had a harp and they were holding golden bowls full of incense, which are the prayers of the saints." ~Revelations 5:8

We have to fill those golden bowls with prayers for our neighbors.

It is also the responsibility of the cell leaders to recruit more intercessors into their team. It must be made clear that joining the prayer movement is not shifting allegiance from the church. Our focus should remain that of building prayer movements that are full of faithful people that submit to the authorities of their respective churches. We do not entertain rebellious people on our teams because their presence will just hinder our prayers from getting answered by God.

Prayer cell leaders are to meet regularly with the prayer coordinator for evaluation. As a team, the prayer coordinator, together with prayer cell leaders keep injecting new ideas on how to expand the prayer movement. In our case, Eunice came up with the idea of picking 'secret friends' and praying for them for one month. In doing this, names of the members are written on small pieces of papers and then they are folded. People are then asked to pick any of the folded pieces of paper randomly. The person you pick becomes your secret prayer friend for a whole month. No one is to know who his or her secret prayer friend is until the day for revealing it. By just meeting and chatting with the person you are meant to pray for, you are supposed to get prayer ideas. After the month is up, people gather to reveal whom they were praying for, and every one buys a gift to bless those they were praying for. The gift does not have to be expensive because it will discourage those who cannot afford one. During the revealing of the secret prayer friends, people share what they experienced during the month and what God did. It is a good idea to serve snacks during the revealing day if you can afford it, but do not overstretch yourself.

Many people have joined our prayer movement because of the many creative ways of recruitment that we have employed. We must, however, keep focus so that the movement does not become a fun club devoid of prayer.

We are the ones that stand in the gap on behalf of the people.

I looked for a man among them who would build up the wall and stand before me in the gap on behalf of the land so I would not have to destroy it, but I found none. ~Ezekiel 22:30

Spiritual Warfare

The reason for building prayer movements is so that we

can invade the camp of the enemy and rescue those that have been taken captive by the devil.

We are engaged in spiritual warfare, and the battle line is already drawn—it is believers versus the forces of the wicked one. It is a battle for the souls of men and women. Many people do not want to hear that there is a devil to be fought and this is like an ostrich hiding its head in the sand thinking that it will not be seen—it is wishful thinking.

One good thing about the war we are involved in is that we are not operating on the same footing with the devil. We are more than conquerors through Christ who strengthens us.

What, then, shall we say in response to this? If God is for us, who can be against us? He who did not spare his own Son, but gave him up for us all—how will he not also, along with him, graciously give us all things? Who will bring any charge against those whom God has chosen? It is God who justifies. Who is he that condemns? Christ Jesus, who died—more than that, who was raised to life—is at the right hand of God and is also interceding for us. Who shall separate us from the love of Christ? Shall trouble or hardship or persecution or famine or nakedness or danger or sword? As it is written: "For your sake we face death all day long; we are considered as sheep to be slaughtered." No, in all these things we are more than conquerors through him who loved us. ~Romans 8:31-37

This is the only battle I know of where the winner is already known before the battle is over. The battle for souls of men has a time framework, and the Bible instructs us to redeem the time because the days are evil. Thousands of people are dying every second and many of them are going to be eternally separated from our God. This knowledge that many are going to hell should make us see the urgency for praying for the salvation of people and preaching the gospel to them.

I remember vividly what happened in December, 2004 while attending our triune event in Port Elizabeth, South Africa. We were scheduled to go and share the gospel one on one in a neighborhood. We took off in a number of buses to the nearby estate and as we arrived at our target area ready to preach, we found a man lying in a pool of blood—an accident had just happened, and the man was dead. Steve Douglass (President of Campus Crusade for Christ) reminded us of the connection of the man's death and the urgency of preaching the gospel. Even as I am writing now, people are dying in different parts of the world.

Even when there is limited time, pray anyway. I remember some years back while a student in college, I visited my brother Peter with whom we went to visit a cousin in Kibera slum (one of the largest slums in East and Central Africa). Around the same time, war broke out between Luos and Nubians in the slum. It is very difficult to differentiate those two tribes since they are the same in facial appearance and body complexion. Houses were burnt and people killed. When we realized that things were out of control, we decided it was time to move out of the slum and get back to college. After walking about 500 meters, people suddenly from nowhere surrounded Peter and me. They were properly armed and talking to us in a language we did not know. I decided to silently pray in my heart for God to intervene and save our lives. I found myself going past these people, and they did not notice me leaving. I am persuaded to date that God blinded these people. These people started beating Peter and left him hurriedly, thinking he was dead. We came to realize later on that these people were Nubians and that in order to differentiate Nubians and those who are not, they were speaking in their mother tongue. If you did not respond, they would slash you to death. A number of people lost their lives on that day alone. As I moved past those people, I kept praying that God would deliver Peter. God answered my prayer — Peter was beaten up, but it was not that bad especially after we massaged him.

This episode reminded me of 2 Kings 6:18: *As the enemy came down toward him, Elisha prayed to the Lord, "Strike these people with blindness." So he struck them with blindness, as Elisha had asked.*

Through the prayer movement, God has been doing great things in our region, some of which I may not share in this book given the nature of their sensitivity. Ask God to give you favor with pastors so that they can be a part of the prayer movement.

I request you to go in prayer before the Master and ask him to help you know how best you can come up with a prayer movement in your area. Ask God to bring into the movement humble servants who have a great desire to see the ruler ship and the Lordship of Christ established in your area.

To support Ken and his family through prayer, read his updates posted at:

http://www.expectationmissions.org

To support Ken and his family financially, please send funds…

In America:

Campus Crusade for Christ

Attn: Donation Center

100 Lake Hart Dr. Dept. 2400

Orlando, FL 32832-0100

Designate giving to:

Acct #: 2819742 – Kennedy Ochieng Okello

In Africa:

Life Ministry

C/O Kennedy Ochieng Okello

PO Box 62500

00100

Nairobi

All funds go directly to Ken, via Campus Crusade for Christ, to support Ken, family, and the ministry in Garissa and Dadaab, Kenya.

www.ingramcontent.com/pod-product-compliance
Lightning Source LLC
LaVergne TN
LVHW090949080826
845145LV00003B/951

* 9 7 8 0 6 1 5 1 4 4 4 0 5 *